Johann Wolfgang von Goethe

# TALES FOR
# TRANSFORMATION

Translated by Scott Thompson

D1121207

City Lights Books
San Francisco

© 1987 by Scott Thompson

The illustrations on the cover and on the page preceding the first story are from *Michael Maier's Atalanta Fugiens Sources of an Alchemical Book of Emblems* by H. M. E. de Jong.

Designed by Patricia Fujii
2nd Printing, 1991

Library of Congress Cataloging-in-Publication Data

Goethe, Johann Wolfgang von, 1749-1832.
  Tales for transformation.

  1. Goethe, Johann Wolfgang von, 1749-1832—
Translations, English, I. Title.
PT2027 .A2T46  1987    833'.6    87-2980
ISBN: 0-87286-211-9 (pbk.)

A special thanks to Dennis Jakob for suggesting a City Lights edition of "Märchen" and for the loan of material from his Goethe collection.

City Lights Books are available to bookstores through our primary distributor: Subterranean Company. P. O. Box 168, 265 S. 5th St., Monroe, OR 97456. 503-847-5274. Toll-free orders 800-274-7826. FAX 503-847-6018. Our books are also available through library jobbers and regional distributors. For personal orders and catalogs, please write to City Lights Books, 261 Columbus Avenue, San Francisco CA 94133.

CITY LIGHTS BOOKS are edited by Lawrence Ferlinghetti and Nancy J. Peters and published at the City Lights Bookstore, 261 Columbus Avenue, San Francisco, CA 94133.

# *Table of Contents*

# Introduction

*. . . where the sacred harmony springs from life itself and where
life evolves according to the principle of harmony . . . only here
will spirit and senses develop a receptive and cultivating power
within the happy symmetry which is the soul of beauty and
the condition of humanity.*

*— Schiller*

Sparks from the athanor, the Vase of Hermes, flicker in and out
of these tales about self-mastery and transformation, for the incuba-
tion of Genius was the Great Work of Goethe's early aesthetic educa-
tion. In 1768, at the age of 19, he and his friend Susannah von Klet-
tenberg began to study the hermetic literature suggested by a Pietist
doctor whose alchemical powder had effected Goethe's recovery from
a severe illness. In the following years, Goethe immersed himself in
the Hermetic tradition, studying Georg von Welling's *Opus mago-
cabalisticum*, the works of Paracelsus, Basilius Valentinus, von
Helmont, Starkey and others. He read from the Kabbalah,
Neoplatonism, Gnosticism, the writings of Jacob Boehme, Heinrich
Khunrath, Cornelius Agrippa and Nostradamus. He even set up an
alchemical laboratory and attempted to make an elixir of immortality.

Although he eventually gave up his empirical alchemical experi-
ments, he was to believe in the validity of the Great Work for the rest
of his life.

Alchemical symbolism is prominent in many of his works, in-
cluding *Faust*, and it is particularly abundant in the first tale of this
collection "Fairy Tale" ("Märchen"). In his *Goethe the Alchemist*,
Ronald Gray presents an alchemical interpretation of this story in
which the River is the Hermetic Stream, the marriage of the Lily and
the Youth represents the *mysterium coniunctionis*, Lily herself is the
Philosopher's Stone, the Will-o'-the-wisps "must surely be the *Aurum*

i

## Introduction

Potabilus of Paracelsus" and so on. The theosophist Rudolph Steiner and the Jungian psychologist Alice Raphael (*Goethe and the Philosopher's Stone*) have also written related analyses of this enigmatic tale that has inspired a whole literature of interpretation. After reading J. V. Andrea's *Chymical Wedding of Christian Rosencreutz*, Goethe wrote to his friend Charlotte von Stein that "there will be a good fairy tale to tell at the right time, but it will have to be reborn, it can't be enjoyed in its old skin." Whether or not this was the inspiration for Goethe's "Märchen," Goethe himself called the story "a fairy tale that will remind you of everything and nothing," and he refused to divulge its meaning "until 99 others had failed to do so."

"Fairy Tale" is the last narrative in *Conversations of German Emigrants*, a cycle of stories told by the aristocracy who had been driven from their homes during the tumultuous years of the Revolution. Goethe did not intend to stir up revolutionary fervor but to temper unleashed passions and, because his own aristocratic conservatism was out of step with the times, his book did not find popular favor. Though he wrote against sans-culottism, Goethe was also committed to the liberation of the human soul. Repelled by the violent atrocities of the Reign of Terror, both he and Schiller who published the stories in installments in the journal *Die Horen* proposed the Pythagorean principle of harmony and the disinterested appreciation of beauty as the prerequisites for a transition to a free society. Aesthetic education was to be the foundation of a truly moral social order in which individuals could unfold their latent capabilities in an organic way. Today, as liberal education becomes replaced by the legitimating program of corporate techno-barbarism, reducing subjectivity to colonized appetites, Goethe's idea of education stands totally opposed to the American false consciousness that Brecht once called "the mausoleum of easy going."

From *Conversations*, too, is "The Counselor," a subtle adaptation of a 15th-century French story about a young wife's struggle to overcome the temptation of illicit passion. It is an excellent example of the "moral tale," the name given by Goethe to the genre before the term "novelle" came into use. In comic contrast to "The Counselor," "The New Melusina" offers a parallel story of temptation, this time about an intemperate man who is fascinated by a woman whose every test he fails. Goethe had probably read Paracelsus's *De pygmaeis*, which introduces the idea of a mercurial melusina who has the power to change shape and to cure. Goethe's version of this universal folk theme is among the best, and he is said to have enjoyed reading it aloud to small audiences throughout his life.

The harmonious reconciliation of polar opposites is a striking motif in many of Goethe's stories, and the relationship between man and woman frequently serves as matrix for a finally attained balance. In "The Good Women," a discussion among six writers and artists illustrates some of Goethe's views on the cultivation of aesthetic sensibility and the power of art to attune the soul to a loftier music. Here, too, is a good example of Goethe's trope of the Amazon, the perfect blend of male and female so reminiscent of the alchemical androgyne.

Defending the rights of women, the character Armidoro presents Goethe's own view when he says "there's no question that in all civilized nations, women must gain superiority; for in reciprocity, the man must become the feminine and this is a loss to him because his merit is not in moderate but in disciplined strength. Yet if a woman acquires something from a man, it's to her advantage, for if she can better her position with energy, the result is a being which could not be more perfect."

"Novelle," Goethe's finest short work of prose, was begun as a lyrical poem (the poem appears as a song within the completed tale), but it was not published until thirty years later, in 1828. This tale about the taming of the passions is both the example of and a statement on the classical German novelle. Here, the contradictions between nature and art, emotion and reflection, barbarism and civilization are ultimately resolved in "the sacred harmony that springs from life itself." As in many works by Goethe, the attainment of symmetry and repose is suggested through music. Only when music speaks to the unworthy lover of the "New Melusina," is he finally able to understand his errors. In "Novelle," Prince and Princess come together, and all are momentarily reconciled as the gypsy boy plays his flute:

*Everyone seemed tempered, each heart touched in its own way. The Prince, as if only now able to overlook the trouble*

*which had threatened him earlier, looked down at his wife.*
*...A perfect silence ruled the crown and the dangers...*
*seemed to have been forgotten.*

Goethe began to write a sequel to Mozart's opera *The Magic Flute* in 1795, and he intended to use the same characters, the same actors, costumes, and stage decor so that audiences would have no difficulty making the transition. In January of the following year, he asked his friend Paul Wranitzky to compose the music. However, various complications arising out of the continuing performance of the original opera forced Wranitzky to decline his offer. Karl Aelter, another friend, who set a number of poems by Goethe and Schiller to music, seemed to be interested but had actually misunderstood the offer, thinking he was being asked to compose new music for the original *Magic Flute* instead of Goethe's sequel.

The fragment, as it now stands, was essentially completed in 1795, though some emendations were made three years later. The song beginning "of all the pretty wares" was published separately in Johann Voss's *Musenalmanach* of 1796. The bookdealer, Friedrich Wilmans, published the complete text in 1802 with the intention of helping Goethe find a composer, but no music was ever composed for the piece, even though Goethe pursued the project on and off for twenty years.

Emanuel Schikaneder, Mozart's librettist, drew from two earlier sources: Liebeskind's *Lulu oder die Zauberflöte* (*Lulu or the Magic Flute*) of 1789 and Pater Terrasson's French novel, *Sethos, histoire ou vie tirée des monumens anecdotes de l'ancienne Egypte; traduit d'un manuscript Grec*, of 1731, (*The Life of Sethos, taken from private Memoirs of the Ancient Egyptian; translated from a Greek Manuscript into French and now done into English by M. Lediard*). The novel details the trials and initiations of a young Egyptian prince into the mysteries of Isis, Osiris, and Horus, and its mystical content provided Schikaneder and Mozart (both of them Freemasons) with the opportunity of bringing Masonic pageantry to the Viennese stage. The essential idea of the opera was the triumph of light over darkness, a Masonic theme developed through Pythagorean number mysticism: three lodge officers, three years of novitiate, three great and small lights at the lodge's entrance, three knocks at the door, three ground pillars, the Queen's three attendant women, the three slaves, three corporeal and three spiritual trials, and so on.

Goethe's sequel takes its inspiration from a moment in Schikaneder's story when the evil Monostatos, unable to win Pamina's love, has joined forces with the Queen of the Night in order to gain Pamina's hand as a reward. Monostatos returns, having stolen Pamina and Tamino's child and imprisoned him in a golden sarcophagus which, however, proves to be too heavy to lift. Monostatos then seals it shut with the Queen's seal. To this is added the Queen's curse: should Pamina and Tamino look at each other, they'd go mad; and should they see their child, he would die. The story culminates with the reunification of the King and Queen and the liberation of Genius, their child. The trial by water and fire at the close of the piece derives from the Sethos novel and the initiation into the mysteries of Isis and Osiris.

Scholars have found in the capture and liberation of Genius intimations of the Euphorion-Faust-Helen scene in *Faust II*; and the dialogue between the two watchmen at the close of the fragment has been likened to the dialogue between the subterranean kings and the Old Man with the lamp in Goethe's "Fairy Tale."

Goethe's friend, Karl Ludwig Knebel, expressed his admiration: "Goethe has painted delicate and penetrating hieroglyphics in his second part of the *Magic Flute*." Those who are interested in Goethe's Masonic involvement will find this unusual opera fragment worth deeper study. Goethe, speaking to Eckermann, remarked: "the higher sense (of the Magic Flute II) will not elude the initiated." Whether or not the reader is an adept of higher orders, this tale of transformation, liberated genius and the magical nature of music may strike a sympathetic chord and illuminate this lesser known aspect of the last renaissance titan, Europe's greatest man of letters.

—Scott Thompson

EPIGRAMMA XXI.

# ☾ Fairy Tale (Märchen) ☽

BY the great river, swollen and inundated with a recent heavy rain, the old Ferryman, worn out by the day's work, lay asleep in his little hut. In the middle of the night, loud voices woke him up; he overheard travelers wanting to be transported.

As he stepped to the doorway, he saw two large Will-o'-the-wisps* floating above the docked boat. They declared that they were in a rush and wished that they were already on the yonder bank. Without delay, the old man pushed off and steered across the stream with his customary adroitness while the strangers rasped at each other in a highly spirited and unknown tongue, occasionally bursting out in a loud cachinnation as they bounced back and forth from the seats and sides to the bottom of the boat.

"The boat's rocking!" shouted the old man, "and if you're too unruly it can tip over; sit down, Herr Radiants!"*

They burst out in loud cackling at this order, hooted at the old man, and were more disruptive than ever. He patiently endured their vexations and they soon reached the other bank.

"Here's something for your trouble!" yelled the travelers, and as they shook themselves, many glittering gold pieces fell into the damp boat.

"What in God's name are you doing!" shouted the old man, "you'll bring me the worst bad luck! If a gold piece fell in the water, terrible waves would rise up and swallow me and my boat, and who knows what would happen to you. The stream can't abide this metal, take your money back!"

"We can't take back anything we've shaken off," they replied.

---

*The English word will-o'-the-wisp does not convey the full sense of the German Irrlicht—irr (errant), licht (light). Transl.

1

"Then you cause me the additional trouble of gathering them together and carrying them to shore to bury," said the old man as he bent down and collected the gold pieces in his cap.

As the Will-o'-the-wisps sprang out of the boat, the old man cried after them, "Where's my pay?"

"Who takes no gold, works for free!" they shouted back.

"Surely you know that I can only be paid in fruits of the earth."

"With fruits of the earth? We not only detest them, we've never even tasted them."

"But I can't let you go until you promise to bring me three heads of cabbage, three artichokes, and three large onions."

The Will-o'-the-wisps would have gleefully slipped away, but they felt themselves inexplicably stuck to the ground; it was the most unpleasant sensation they had ever had. They promised to comply with his demand as soon as they could. He released them and pushed off. He was far off in the distance when they yelled after him: "Old man! Listen, old man! We've forgotten the most important thing!" But he was gone and didn't hear them. He had drifted further down the same side of the river, where he wanted to conceal the dangerous gold in a mountainous region never reached by the water. There he found a vast cleft between towering boulders where he cast away the gold. Then he returned to his hut.

The beautiful green Snake was in this cleft, and the falling jangle of coins woke her from her sleep. Having barely discerned the sparkling discs, she now gulped them down voraciously and then zealously sought the pieces which had been scattered in the bushes and crevices.

No sooner had she swallowed them than she felt the most pleasant sensation of gold melting in her innards and radiating through her entire body. With the greatest delight, she realized that she had become translucent and illuminated. She had long been assured that this phenomenon was possible, but since she doubted whether this light could last, curiosity and the desire to secure her future propelled her from the rock to find the one who could have cast the gold. She found no one. It was all the more pleasant, then, to admire herself as she glided through plants and thickets, diffusing her graceful light through the fresh green. All the leaves appeared smaragdine and all

2

the flowers were most gloriously transfigured. In vain she wandered through the lonely wilderness; but her hope grew stronger when she came upon a plain and saw a glow like her own in the distance. "I've found my complement after all!" she cried, and hurried to the place. She noticed no difficulty as she crawled through swamp and reed, though she preferred to live on dry mountain meadows and in high rocky fissures, savouring spicy herbs and quenching her thirst with fine dew and fresh spring water. But she would have accepted any undertaking for the sake of the coveted gold and the glorious light.

Extremely weary, she finally reached a damp marsh where our two Will-o'-the-wisps were skipping back and forth. She rushed up to greet them, overjoyed to find such agreeable gentlemen among her relations. The Lights strolled up and hopped over her, laughing in their usual manner. "Frau Cousin," they said, "though you are of the horizontal lineage, it doesn't matter; of course, we're only related on the glowing side. You can see how handsomely this slender length suits us gentlemen of the vertical lineage." (With this, both flames elongated, making themselves as tall and pointed as they could," completely sacrificing their width.) "Don't get us wrong, dear friend. What family can boast of such an honor? As long as there have been Will-o'-the-wisps, not one has sat or reclined."

The Snake felt quite uncomfortable in the presence of these relatives, for no matter how high she raised her head, she felt she must bend it to the earth to make any progress, and though earlier she'd felt extraordinarily pleased with herself in the dark grove, her luster seemed to diminish with each second in the presence of these cousins and she was afraid that it would completely go out.

In her embarrassment, she quickly asked whether the gentlemen could tell her the origin of the gold which had fallen into the mountain cleft; she supposed that a gold rain had trickled directly from heaven. The Will-o'-the-wisps laughed and shook, and a heap of gold pieces jingled down around them. Darting after them, the Snake gobbled them up. "Bon appetit, Frau Cousin," said the kindly gentlemen. "Would you like more?" They jiggled again a couple of times so quickly that the Snake could barely swallow the costly repast fast enough. Her shiny appearance began to glow and she sparkled with a truly glorious luminescence, while the Will-o'-the-wisps seemed to be come meager and smaller, though their good dispositions weren't the least diminished.

"I'm forever in your debt," said the Snake, recovering her breath after feasting. "Ask of me whatever you wish. If it's in my power, I'll satisfy your request."

"Splendid!" exclaimed the Will-o'-the-wisps. "Where can the beautiful Lily be found? Lead us as quickly as possible to the palace and garden of the beautiful Lily. We're dying of impatience to fling ourselves at her feet."

"I cannot perform this service at once," replied the Snake with a deep sigh. "Unfortunately, the beautiful Lily lives beyond the water."

"Beyond the water! And we let ourselves be transported here in this stormy night! How terrifying this river is that now separates us! Can't we call the old man back?"

"You'd trouble yourselves for nothing," answered the Snake, "for even if you met him on this side of the river, he still wouldn't take you. He may bring everyone across, but no one back."

"What a fine fix we've concocted! Is there no other way, then, to cross the water?"

"There are a few, but nothing can be done this instant. I can transport you myself, but only during the hour of noon."

"That's a time when we don't like to travel."

"Then you can ride across on the giant's shadow in the evening."

"How's that done?"

"Not far from here lives a great giant whose body is powerless; his hands can't lift a single straw, his shoulders can't carry a twig, but his shadow can do a lot, everything in fact. That's why he's strongest at sunrise and sunset. At evening you have only to sit on the neck of his shadow, and when the giant slowly walks to the river bank, his shadow brings you across the water. But if you show up at noon at the edge of that wood where the bushes hang thick over the bank, I can transport you and present you to the beautiful Lily; if you're hesitant about the noon heat, you can call on the giant around evening in that rocky cove. I'm sure he'll accommodate you."

With a parting bow, the young gentlemen withdrew into the distance. The Snake was glad to get away too, not only to bask in her own light, but also to satisfy a curiosity which had particularly tormented her for a long time.

In the rock clefts where she often slinked about, she'd discovered something very peculiar. Though circumstances necessitated that she crawl through these abysses without a light, with her sense of touch she could nonetheless distinguish objects quite well. Accustomed to finding only the irregular works of nature, she'd wind in and out of the jagged edges of great crystals, coiling through the snags and veins of pure silver, now and then drawing other precious stones along with her into the light. Yet to her great amazement, she also touched upon some objects in a grotto which betrayed the fabricating hand of man. Here were smooth walls she could not scale, sharp, regular corners, well-constructed columns and, most unusual of all, human figures around which she'd spiralled more than once, and which she supposed to be of bronze or extremely polished marble. With her sense of sight, she now wished to unite all these experiences and to confirm what before she'd only guessed. She now believed herself capable of illuminating this wonderful subterranean vault with her own light, and hoped to be wholly familiar with these peculiarities soon. Hurrying along her usual path, she found the crevice through which she had slipped into the sanctuary.

When she reached the spot, she looked around with curiosity and although her light did not illuminate everything in the rotunda, the objects closest to her were perceptible. Astonished and humbled, she stared up at a glittering niche where the imposing likeness of a king stood fixed in pure gold. In measure, the statue was larger than life-size, but its form represented a short rather than a tall man. Its finely proportioned body was draped with a simple cloak, and an oak garland kept his hair in place.

The Snake had barely set eyes upon this august image when the king began to speak. "Where do you come from?" he asked.

"From the clefts where the gold is lodged," replied the Snake.

"What's more magnificent than gold?" asked the King.

"Light," answered the Snake.

"What's more exhilarating than light?" he asked.

"Speech," she answered.

During this exchange, she cast a sideways glance into the next niche where she spied another majestic image. A silver king with a tall and slender form sat there. His body was veiled by an ornamented robe, crown, girdle, and a scepter decorated with jewels. He wore the jubilance of self-esteem on his face and seemed about to speak when a dark-colored vein running along the marble wall suddenly brightened, and a felicitous light spilled out through the whole temple. The Snake saw a third king in this light. His mighty bronze frame leaned there upon his club, and he was adorned with a laurel wreath. He looked more like a boulder than a man. She turned to look for the fourth king, who was the most distant from her, but as the brilliant vein flashed like a lightning bolt and vanished, the wall opened.

A man of medium height stepped out, drawing the Snake's attention to himself. He was in peasant's garb, and in his hand he carried a small lamp with a quiet flame, pleasing to the eye, that lit up the entire dome without casting a single shadow.

"As we have light already, what brings you here?" asked the golden king.

"You know that I may not enlighten the darkness."

"Will my kingdom end?" asked the silver king.

"Late or never," replied the old man.

"When will I ascend?" asked the bronze king with a powerful voice.

"Soon," replied the old man.

"With whom shall I be united?" asked the king.

"With your older brothers," said the old man.

"What will become of the youngest?" asked the king.

"He will take his seat," said the old man.

"I'm not tired," the fourth king cried out with a hoarse and faltering voice.

While they spoke, the Snake had slid quietly around the temple, scanning everything, at last spotting the fourth king nearby. As he stood leaning on a pillar, his stately frame more awkward than handsome, it was not easy to distinguish the metal in which he'd been cast. On close examination, it was a mixture of the three metals which made up his brothers, though these materials did not appear to have been properly forged together. Gold and silver veins traveled irregularly through a mass of bronze, giving the figure an unpleasant appearance.

The golden king then asked the man, "How many secrets do you know?"

"Three," replied the old man.

"Which is the most important?" asked the silver king.

"The revealed one," replied the old man.

"Will you divulge it to us?" asked the bronze king.

"As soon as I know the fourth one," said the old man.

"What do I care!" mumbled the synthetic king.

"I know the fourth," said the Snake, approaching the old man and hissing something in his ear.

"The time has come!" shouted the old man with a booming voice. The temple resounded, the metal statues rang out, and in that instant the old man sank toward the west, the Snake toward the east, both of them slipping through the clefts in the rocks with great speed.

All the passages through which the old man wandered were instantly filled behind him with gold, for his lamp had the wonderful quality of transmuting stones into gold, wood into silver, dead animals into jewels; and it could shatter all metals. To manifest these changes, it had to shine entirely by itself. Were another light brought into contact with it, it produced only a nice bright shine, but one that nonetheless quickened all living things.

The old man stepped into his mountain hut and found his wife in the direst straits. She sat by the fire crying and could not be consoled. "I'm so miserable," she lamented. "Didn't I tell you not to leave today?"

"What happened?" asked the old man very quietly.

"You were hardly out of sight when two boisterous wanderers knocked on the door," she sobbed. "Without thinking, I let them in. They seemed like two well-behaved and proper young men. They were dressed in light flames; you would've thought they were two Will-o'-the-wisps. Scarcely had they set foot in the house when they began to flatter me in the most insolent manner, and they became so impertinent that the very thought of it humiliates me."

"Obviously they were fooling," said the old man with a smile. "With respect to your age, they should have observed a little common courtesy."

"Age! What age?" shouted the wife. "Do I always have to hear about my age? How old am I, then? Common courtesy! Yet I know what I know. Just look around at the walls. Look at those old stones that I hadn't seen in ages. They licked off all the gold so fast you would hardly have believed it; and they kept assuring me that it tasted much better than common gold. When they'd scoured the walls bare, they seemed to be in a highly spirited mood and, to be sure, they grew a lot taller, broader, and more irradiant than ever. That's when they began their mischief again, caressing me and calling me their queen. Then they danced around shaking these gold pieces all over the place. See them sparkling there under the bench? What bad luck! Our Mops ate a few of them and look, there he lies by the fireplace, dead. The poor creature! I'll never get over it. Had I seen him there before they left, I'd never have promised to pay off their debt to the Ferryman."

"What do they owe him?" asked the old man.

"Three heads of cabbage, three artichokes, and three onions," said the wife. "I promised to bring them to the river by daybreak."

"You can do them this service," said the old man, "for they'll eventually return the favor as well."

"Whether they return the favor, I don't know, but they promised and vowed that they would."

Meanwhile, the fire in the hearth had burned out. The old man covered the coals with ashes and brushed the sparkling gold pieces to the side. Once again, his lamp burned alone. Its dazzling luminescence spread a golden sheen across the wall, changing Mops into the most beautiful onyx imaginable. The alternating brown and black colors of the precious gem made it the most exceptional work of art.

"Put the onyx in your basket, then set the three heads of cabbage, three artichokes, and three onions around it, and carry it to the river," said the old man. "Around noon, let the Snake transport you to visit the beautiful Lily. Bring her the onyx, for just as her touch kills every living thing, it also brings the dead back to life. She'll find a true companion in the dog. Tell her not to weep, her liberation approaches. She can look upon her misfortune as a blessing in disguise, for the time has come."

The old woman packed her basket and started off along the path at daybreak. The rising sun was shining brightly on the river, which glistened in the distance. The woman took slow steps, for the basket weighed heavily upon her head, though it wasn't the onyx that weighed her down. The dead things in her basket were no burden, and when they were her only load, the basket rose up in the air and hovered over her head. But a fresh legume or small living animal was extremely heavy to carry. Having wandered disagreeably but a short stretch, she suddenly stood still with fright. She had stepped on the giant's shadow, which extended toward her all the way across the plain.

When she saw the terrible giant step from his bath in the river, she didn't know how she would pacify him. As soon as he noticed her, he greeted her facetiously, and the hand of his shadow grabbed her basket. With accomplished ease, she took out a head of cabbage, an artichoke, and an onion, and put them into the mouth of the giant, who then walked off upstream, leaving the path free for her to continue.

Wondering whether she should return to her garden to replace the missing pieces, she hesitated but pressed on. Her doubts remained with her until she reached the bank of the river. There she sat a long time, waiting for the Ferryman. She finally saw him approaching with an exceptional traveler. A young, noble, handsome man stepped out of the boat. She could not take her eyes off of him.

"What brings you?" shouted the old man.

"These vegetables, which the Will-o'-the-wisps owe you," replied the woman, pointing to her basket. Finding only two of each kind, the old man became annoyed and assured her that he would not be able to take her. The woman pleaded with him. She told him that she was now unable to return home and that her load would prove overbearing for the path still ahead. But he stood firm in his refusal and assured her that the decision was really not his to make.

"Whatever compensation I receive must be left untouched for nine hours, and I can't take anything until I've delivered a third of it to the river." After much haggling back and forth, the old man answered. "There is still one last resort. If you'll answer to the river yourself and declare your own indebtedness, I'll take these six pieces, but there is a risk involved."

"Will I run the risk if I keep my word?"

"Not at all. Stick your hand in the river," continued the old man, "and promise that you'll settle the debt in twenty-four hours."

The old woman complied, but as she drew her hand from the water she was horrified to find it black as coal. She railed loudly at the old man, affirming that her hands had always been her finest features and that she had intentionally kept these noble limbs white and delicate despite all her hard work. She looked at her hand with great dismay and cried out in despair. "This is even worse! See, it's disappearing; it's become much smaller than the other."

"It only appears so for the moment," said the old man; "but if you don't keep your word, it may really happen. Your hand will gradually disappear until it completely vanishes, though you won't be deprived of its use. You'll be able to do everything as before, with the one exception that no one will be able to see your hand."

"I'd rather not use it at all than have people think it missing," said the old woman, "but, so what, I'll keep my word and soon shake off this black skin and all these worries." She quickly picked up her basket, which raised itself above her head and hovered freely in the air, and hurried after the pensive young man, who wandered quietly down the bank. His handsome figure and curious attire had deeply impressed her.

Each line of his beautiful body rippled through the shiny mail that covered his chest. A purple cape hung around his shoulders; from his uncovered head wavy brown hair flowed in beautiful locks; his pleasing face was exposed to the sun's rays as were his well-proportioned feet. He walked calmly upon the hot sand with bare soles, and a deep sorrow seemed to dull him to all external impressions.

The talkative old woman tried to converse with him, but his curt replies were uninformative and discouraging. Despite his lovely eyes she finally tired of speaking in vain and bid him farewell saying "You walk too slowly for me, sir. I haven't a moment to lose because I must cross the river on the green Snake and present the beautiful Lily this fine gift from my husband." With these words, she hurried off, but the handsome youth quickened his stride, hastening to keep up with her pace.

"You're going to the beautiful Lily?" he shouted. "Then we're on the same path. What kind of gift is this you're carrying?"

"My dear man," replied the old woman, "it's improper to ask about my secrets so inquisitively when you've dismissed my questions so curtly. However, if you'll trade, and tell me your fate, I won't hide the story of myself and my gift from you." And so they agreed. The woman divulged her situation along with the story of the dog, and allowed him to see the wonderful gift.

He promptly lifted the natural work of art from the basket and took Mops, who seemed to be resting quietly, in his arms. "Lucky dog!" he exclaimed. "The touch of her hand will revive you, though the living flee her presence to escape a sorrowful fate. But why do I say sorrowful? Isn't it even more miserable and terrible to be wounded by her gaze than to die by her hand? Look at me," he said to the old woman, "I've already suffered quite a wretched misfortune at my age! Fate has dealt me this armor, which I've worn proudly into battle, and this purple, which I tried to earn by ruling wisely: the one is an unnecessary burden and the other is a meaningless ornament. Crown, scepter, and sword are gone; and I'm just as naked and needy as any other son of earth. Lily's beautiful blue eyes are so unhappy that they enfeeble every living being they look on, and those not killed by her touch are left to wander as living shadows."

So he continued to lament, which by no means satisfied the old woman's curiosity. She preferred to hear more about his external circumstances and less about his internal disposition. She learned neither his father's name nor the name of his kingdom. He stroked the petrified Mops, whom the rays of sun and his own breast had warmed, as if the pug were alive. He asked many questions about the man with the lamp, the effects of its holy light, and he seemed to foresee a great benefit from it for his misfortune.

In the middle of this exchange, they spotted the majestic arch of the bridge in the distance. Its expanse shimmered most strangely in the sun's brilliance from one bank to the other. Both of them were astounded. They had never seen this structure look so imposing.

"Wasn't it glorious enough when it towered before us in jasper and agate," cried the Prince? Isn't this melodious appearance of smaragdine, chrysoprase and chrysolite too sublime to set foot upon?"

Neither of them knew of the Snake's transformation, for it was in fact the Snake who spanned the river in the bold form of a bridge every day at noon. The wanderers stepped forth on it in admiration and crossed over in silence.

Just as they reached the other bank, the bridge began to swing back and forth, and as it touched the water's surface, the green Snake glided after them in her characteristic form. They had barely thanked her for the privilege of crossing the river on her back when they noticed that there must be more than three in their company, although they couldn't see anyone else. They heard a hiss next to them which the Snake answered with another hiss. Listening carefully, they were finally able to recognize this conversation between a pair of alternating voices:

"First, we'll look around incognito in the beautiful Lily's park. At night, when we're more presentable, we'll ask you to introduce us to this perfect beauty. You can meet us on the shore of the great lake."

"So be it," replied the Snake, and a hissing vanished into the air.

Our three wanderers now conferred amongst themselves about the order in which they should present themselves to the Beauty, for whatever their numbers, they could only approach her one at a time if they did not want to endure insufferable pain.

The woman holding the basket with the transformed dog entered the garden first and looked around for her patroness, who was easy to find because her voice could be heard singing, accompanied by her harp. The delightful tones first appeared as rings on the surface of the still lake; then, like a light breath, they rippled the grass and bushes into movement. She sat on a secluded green heath overshadowed by a regal group of various trees. As the charmed old woman drew closer, her eyes, ears, and heart were instantly enchanted with the first glimpse of the Beauty, and she swore to herself that Lily had become even more beautiful than ever before. The good woman called out greetings and praise to the charming maiden. "What good fortune to see you! What a paradise your presence emanates! The harp leans in your lap enticed by your gentle arms' embrace. It seems to yearn toward your breast. It sounds so tender under your slender fingers' caress. Thrice-blessed be the youth who could take its place!"

The old woman came closer as she spoke these praises. The beautiful Lily raised her eyelids, letting her hands sink to her side and answered, "Don't depress me with untimely praise. It only deepens my feelings of misfortune. See, the poor canary lies dead at my feet. He had been the most pleasant accompaniment to my songs and had learned to sit on my harp. I trained him not to touch me. As I woke refreshed from sleep this morning and sang a quiet hymn, my little singer trilled his harmonious notes more cheerful than ever. But then a hawk shot down over my head and the poor little creature took flight to my breast, and in that instant I felt the last quiver of his fleeting life. The culprit of course was pierced by my gaze and fluttered helplessly to the water, but what good is vengeance. My beloved is dead and his grave will only add to the unhappy shrubs in my garden."

"Take heart, lovely Lily!" exclaimed the woman as she wiped away a tear which the unhappy maiden's story had brought to her eyes. "Pull yourself together. My husband says that you should restrain your mourning and look upon the greatest misfortune as an omen of the greatest fortune, for the time has come. There is confusion in the world, that's true," she continued. "Look at my hand, how black it's become! It's actually getting smaller, and I must hurry before it completely disappears! Why did I have to do a favor for the Will-o'-the-wisps, why did I have to confront the giant, and why did I ever have to dip my hand in the river? Couldn't you give me a head of cabbage, an artichoke, and an onion? I would in turn give them to the river and my hand would become white again, and I could almost compare it to yours."

"You may still be able to find cabbages and onions, but it's useless to look for any artichokes. No plants in my garden have blossoms or fruit, but every twig I snap off and plant on the grave of one I love immediately greens and shoots up tall. All these shrubs and groves have grown up around my misfortune. The canopies of these pines, the obelisks of these cypresses, the colossal oaks and beeches — all these were once little twigs planted by my hand in an otherwise unfertile earth."

The old woman had paid little attention to this speech and could only stare at her hand which not only grew blacker and blacker in Lily's presence, but also seemed to become smaller by the minute. She wanted to pick up her basket and dash off when she realized that she'd forgotten the most important point of her visit. She immediately picked up the metamorphosed dog and set him in the grass near the Beauty. "My husband sends you this keepsake," she said. "You know that your touch can resuscitate this gem. The friendly and faithful animal will certainly give you much joy, and the sorrow I feel, having lost him, can only be brightened by knowing that he belongs to you."

The beautiful Lily seemed to be both pleased and surprised to see the well-bred creature. "Many signs are conspiring to imbue me with hope, but alas! isn't it a delusion of our nature to imagine that the best is about to happen when we encounter a lot of bad luck."

> What good are these propitious signs?
> The canary's death, the woman's black limb?
> The transformed pug, which onyx confines?
> Did not the lamp deliver him?
> Far from the sweets of human pleasure,
> My only confidant is fret.
> Oh, why isn't the temple by the river?
> Why isn't the bridge built yet?

The good woman had listened impatiently to this song which the beautiful Lily, with her pleasing voice, accompanied with her harp, enchanting all the others present. She was about to leave when she was delayed by the arrival of the green Snake. The Snake had heard the last lines of the song and interceded at once to restore her spirit.

"The prophecy of the bridge is fulfilled!" cried the Snake. "Just ask this good woman how gloriously its arch looks now. The once opaque jasper and agate, which had only allowed light to pass at the margin, is now a transparent gem. No beryl is so clear, no smaragdine so colorful."

"I wish you luck," said Lily, "but forgive me; I don't believe that the prophecy has been fulfilled. The high arc of your bridge only permits travelers on foot, but it's been promised that horses and wagons and all sorts of travelers will be able to pass back and forth at the same time. And hasn't it been prophesied that great columns will rise up by themselves from the river?"

The old woman kept her eyes fixed on her hand. She interrupted the interchange to bid farewell. "Stay a moment longer," said the pretty Lily, "and take my poor canary with you. Ask the lamp to transmute it into a beautiful topaz, which I can revive with my touch just like your good Mops. This shall become my favorite pastime; but hurry as fast as you can because putrefaction will afflict the poor creature when the Sun sets, and that would destroy the delicate composition of its form forever."

The old woman placed the little corpse between soft leaves in the basket, and hurried off.

Resuming their interrupted exchange, the Snake said, "Be that as it may, the temple is built."

"But it's not by the river," replied Lily.

The Snake answered, "I heard the great Word resound in the temple; The time has come."

A pleasing cheerfulness radiated across Lily's face. "Am I hearing these happy words already for the second time today? When will the day come when I hear them a third time?"

She stood up and at once a lovely girl stepped from the foliage to take away her harp. She was followed by another girl who folded the carved ivory taboret where Lily had been sitting, and carried its silver pillow under her arm. A third girl who carried a large parasol with pearl stitching asked Lily if she could accompany her on her promenade. These three maidens were all beautiful and charming beyond words, and yet they only served to heighten the beauty of Lily, for everyone had to admit that her beauty was beyond compare.

Lily had been contentedly eyeing the remarkable Mops all this time. She kneeled down and touched him. Instantly he sprang up. He waggishly leapt about, looking all around him and finally darted in excitement to greet his benefactress. She took him in her arms and pressed him to her. "You're so cold," she cried. "Though you've only half a life in you, you'll always be welcome to me; I will love you tenderly, I will tease you playfully, pet you amiably and press you close to my heart." Then she let him down, chased him away from her and called him back, playing with him so gracefully and frolicking with him in the grass with such innocence that one watched her joy with renewed delight and wished to join her, just as her previous sorrow had attuned every heart to empathy.

This merriment and graceful playfulness were interrupted by the arrival of the sad youth. He entered in his characteristic manner, though the heat of the day seemed to have wearied him more, and in the presence of his beloved he grew paler by the moment. In his hand he carried the hawk which was quiet as a dove, its feathers drooping down.

"It's not friendly to bring the detestable beast before my eyes," cried Lily. "That's the monster who killed my little songbird this morning."

"Don't blame the unfortunate bird!" replied the youth. "Blame yourself and your fate, and permit me to keep my comrade in misery at my side."

Mops continued to tease Lily and she answered her pellucid foundling with the most amiable attention. She clapped her hands to scare him off, then ran after him to draw him near. She tried to catch him when he ran away, and she chased him away when he got close. The young man watched all this silently, and with a growing displeasure. The dog completely disgusted him, but when she took the ugly mutt in her arms, pressing it to her breast, and then kissed its black snout with her heavenly lips, he lost all patience and cried out in despair: "Must I, forced by unlucky circumstance to exist apart from you, perhaps forever, having lost everything including self, must I watch such a perverse monstrosity delight you, claim your affection, and savour your embraces! Do I have to keep wandering back and forth, marking time in circles around this river? No! There's still a spark of the old warrior sleeping in my breast, but it's bursting out right now into its last consuming flame! If stones can take comfort in your breast, may I be changed to stone; if your touch kills, then let me die by your hand."

Speaking these words, he made a violent gesture and the hawk flew out of his hands as he fell against the beautiful Lily. She reached out her arms to hold him off and in so doing touched him all the sooner. Consciousness abandoned him, and she was horrified to feel his splendid weight collapse against her breast. She jumped back with a shriek and the gentle youth slumped lifelessly from her arms to the earth.

The catastrophe had now occurred! Motionless, the sweet Lily stood staring at the lifeless body. Her heart seemed to have stopped beating in her breast, and her eyes were without tears. In vain did Mops try to win her kind affection; the whole world had died with her friend. In dumbfounded despair, she looked for no solace; for what solace could she know?

The Snake was all the more agitated however, seeming to reflect on some rescue, and her peculiar undulations actually served to inhibit the following aftershocks of the calamity for a time. Making a wide circle she surrounded the body, bit the end of her tail with her teeth, and lay there peacefully.

One of Lily's pretty maidservants soon stepped forward with the ivory taboret and beckoned with a friendly gesture for the Beauty to sit down. The second maiden then appeared carrying a flame-colored veil with which she adorned rather than concealed her majesty's head. The third maiden placed the harp in her hands. No sooner had Lily plucked a few notes from the strings of the magnificent instrument than the first maiden returned with a bright round mirror, which she placed in front of Lily, whose reflected glance presented her with the most pleasing image to be found in nature. Grief exalted her beauty, the veil heightened her enchantment, and the harp her gracefulness. As much as one wished to see her sorrowful state altered, all the more did one desire to keep her present image close forever.

Gazing calmly into the looking glass, she soon enticed melting tones from the strings. Her grief appeared to intensify and the strings answered her misery with violent notes. She opened her mouth a few times to sing, but her voice failed her and her sadness soon found release in tears. Two of the maidens supported her in their arms, the harp sank from her lap, and the nimble maid barely caught the instrument, bringing it along with them.

"Who will fetch us the man with the lamp before the sun sets?" the Snake hissed softly but audibly. The maidens looked at each other and Lily's tears streamed down her cheeks. At this moment, the woman with the basket returned.

"I'm lost and deformed for life," she cried out. "See how my hand has nearly disappeared completely; neither the Ferryman nor the giant will transport me since I'm still the river's debtor. I've offered a hundred heads of cabbage and a hundred onions in vain— they'll take no more than the three pieces and there's not a single artichoke to be found in this place."

"Forget your worries and try to help us here," said the Snake. "Perhaps you yourself will be helped in the process. Hurry as fast as you can to find the Will-o'-the-wisps; it's still too bright outside to see them but maybe you'll hear them laughing and flapping. If they hurry, the giant will transport them over the river and they'll be able to find the man with the lamp and dispatch him to us."

The wife hurried as fast as she could, and the Snake seemed just as impatient as Lily for the Wisps' return. Unfortunately, the rays of the setting sun were already gilding the treetops in the thicket and long shadows swept across lake and meadow. The Snake fidgeted impatiently and Lily dissolved in tears.

In this predicament, the Snake peered all around her, for she was afraid that the sun would set any moment and that decay would permeate the magic circle, attacking the youth without mercy. At last she spied the purple-red feathers of the hawk high in the sky. Its breast caught the last rays of sunlight. She shivered with delight at this propitious sign, and she was not deceived. Soon thereafter, the man with the lamp could be seen gliding across the lake as if he were wearing ice skates.

The Snake did not change her position but Lily stood up and called to him; "What good spirit sends you this moment that we desire and need you so?"

"The spirit of the lamp has driven me," replied the old man; "and the hawk guided me here. When I'm needed, my lamp flickers and I look to the sky for a sign; some bird or meteor shows me the region in the heavens where I'm to go. Calm yourself, most lovely maiden! Whether or not I can help I don't know, for one alone cannot help; but only he who unites with many at the right hour. We'll keep the worst at bay and we won't lose hope. Keep your circle closed," he continued, as he turned to the Snake. Then he sat down on a mound of earth next to her and illuminated the dead body. "Bring the canary too, and put it in the circle!" The maidens obeyed his order and took the little corpse from the basket which the old woman had left standing.

The sun had set in the meantime, and as darkness advanced, not only the Snake and the old man's lamp glowed after their fashion, but Lily's veil glowed softly as well, coloring her pale cheeks with a hue of roseate dawn and spreading an unending grace across her white gown. All were looking at one another silently. Sorrow and dismay were tempered by certain hope.

The old woman's entrance with the two lively flames was therefore no unpleasant sight. They must have been extravagant in their absence for they appeared now to be extremely gaunt, but this caused them to behave all the more cordially to the princess and the other maidens. With the greatest confidence, they bandied about a host of commonplaces, and they especially demonstrated their great sensitivity to the charm which the glowing veil diffused over Lily and her entourage. Modestly, the ladies closed their eyes. This praise really did seem to embellish their beauty all the more. Everyone but the old woman was pleased and tranquil. Paying no attention to her husband's assurances that her hand could shrink no further as long as his lamp shone upon it, she declared more than once that, at this rate, the noble limb would have completely disappeared before midnight.

The old man with the lamp had listened attentively to the Will-o'-the-wisps' conversation and was pleased that Lily had been distracted and cheered by it. It was a surprise to all when they realized that midnight had arrived. The old man looked up at the stars and began to speak. "We're all together at this auspicious hour. If each attends to his function and performs his own task, then all individual cares will be resolved in universal happiness in the same way common grief drowns out individual joy."

Once these words had been spoken, a wonderful bustling broke out. Everyone was talking out loud and announcing what they had to do; only the three maidens remained still. One had fallen asleep next to the lamp, another by the parasol, and the third by the chair. No one could blame them, for it was late. The flaming young men, having bestowed a few passing compliments upon the maids, focused their attention solely upon Lily, the prettiest of them all.

"Grasp the mirror," said the old man to the hawk, "and with the first ray of sunlight, illuminate the sleepers and waken them with light reflected from on high."

The Snake, beginning to stir again, dissolved the circle and slowly made its way, coiling in large circles toward the river. The Will-o'-the-wisps paraded after her, as if they were the most earnest flames around. The old woman and her husband picked up the basket, whose soft light had almost gone unnoticed. As they carried it, one on each side, it became larger and brighter. They placed the youth's body into the basket with the canary lying on his chest. The basket raised itself high in the air and hovered over the wife's head, and she followed the Will-o'-the-wisps on foot. The beautiful Lily took Mops in her arms and followed the old woman. The old man with the lamp completed the procession, and the region was bathed by their diverse lights.

As the company approached the river, they were amazed to see it spanned by a lordly arc, through which the beneficent Snake had cleared a shining path. By day the structure's transparent jewels appeared wondrous, but at night its sparkling brilliance was truly astonishing. Its bright circle towered aloft, cutting into the darkness of the heavens. Below, animated beams flickered toward the center and outlined the flexible stability of its expanse. The procession crossed over slowly. From his hut, the Ferryman looked out in amazement and watched the illuminated circle and the procession of strange lights passing over.

Just as their feet touched the other side, the arc began to sway near the water like a wave. The Snake soon crawled onto land, the basket lowered itself to the earth, and the Snake again encircled it. The old man nodded to her and asked, "What's your decision?"

"To sacrifice myself before I'm sacrificed," replied the Snake; "promise me you'll leave no stone on land."

The old man promised, and then said to Lily, "Touch the Snake with your left hand and your beloved with your right." Lily knelt down and touched the Snake and the corpse. Instantly, the prince was revived. He began to stir in the basket and even sat up. Lily wanted to embrace him but the old man had to restrain her. Instead, he helped the youth to his feet and guided him as he stepped from the basket and the circle.

The youth stood up and the canary fluttered to his shoulder. Though there was life in them both, their spirits had yet to return. The prince's eyes were open but saw nothing, at least he seemed to be removed from all he saw. As the amazement over this incident began to subside, they noticed how oddly the Snake had been transformed. Her beautiful and slender body had broken into thousands and thousands of sparkling gems; the old woman had carelessly touched her as she reached for the basket. There was nothing left to see of the Snake's form but a pretty circle of shiny jewels lying in the grass.

The old man began at once to collect the stones into the basket, and his wife helped him in this task. Both of them carried it to a tall mound and he shook the whole load into the river, though the Princess and his wife, who gladly would have kept something of it, were opposed to this. Like blinking stars, the stones drifted with the waves and you couldn't tell whether they lost themselves in the distance or sank beneath the surface.

"Gentlemen," said the old man, bowing respectfully to the Will-o'-the-wisps, "I'll now show you the way and open the passage, but you will do us the greatest service if you open the gates of holiness for us, through which we must enter this time. No one but you can open them for us."

The Will-o'-the-wisps nodded in agreement and stood back. The old man with the lamp walked ahead into the rocks which opened before him. The youth followed at his heels with a mechanical kind of gait. Lily remained in the distance, still and uncertain. Not wanting to stay behind, the old woman stretched out her hand to catch the light from her husband's lamp. The Will-o'-the-wisps then sealed the passage by bending their flame tips together. They appeared to be speaking to one another.

They had been walking but a short distance when they found themselves before a bronze gate whose wings were bolted with a golden lock. At once, the old man beckoned to the Will-o'-the-wisps, who eagerly devoured the bolt and lock with their pointed flames.

The bronze resounded with a clang as the gate flew open, and the dignified images of the kings appeared illuminated by the Lights as they entered the sanctuary. Each one of the party bowed before the dignified monarchs, and the Will-o'-the-wisps especially did not fail to fall over themselves in deference.

After a pause, the gold king asked, "Where do you come from?"

21

"From the world," answered the old man.

"Where are you going?" asked the silver king.

"Into the world," said the old man.

"What do you want from us?" asked the bronze king.

"To accompany you," said the old man.

The compound king was about to speak when the gold king said to the Will-o'-the-wisps who had come too close "Get thee away from me! My gold is not for your palate." They turned to the silver king and clung to him. His robe sparkled, brilliant in their yellow reflection.

"Your presence is welcome but I can't feed you. Satisfy your craving somewhere else and bring me your light." They stepped back and slipped past the bronze king, who didn't seem to notice them, and latched on to the compound king.

"Who will rule the world?" he shouted with a shaky voice.

"Whoever stands on two feet," replied the old man.

"*C'est moi!*" said the compound king.

"It shall be revealed," said the old man, "for the time has come." The beautiful Lily threw her arms around the old man's neck and kissed him affectionately. "Holy father, thank you a thousand times," she said. "This is the third time I've heard that fateful word." She had barely spoken when she was forced to hold on to the old man as the ground began to rock beneath them. The old man and the youth also grabbed on to each other. Only the fluttering Will-o'-the-wisps noticed nothing.

The whole temple was clearly moving like a ship slowly drifting from the harbor when the anchor has been hauled in. The depths of the earth seemed to open up as the temple sailed along. No rocks blocked its path; it collided with nothing.

For a few moments, a light rain seemed to trickle through the cupola's opening; the old man held the beautiful Lily tighter and said to her, "We're under the river and we'll soon reach our destination." Shortly thereafter, they believed that they had come to a standstill, but they were deceived; the temple was ascending.

A strange din was now to be heard above their heads. Boards and rafters began to crash chaotically through the opening of the cupola. Lily and the old woman leaped to the side, and the man with the lamp grabbed the youth and stood still. The temple had sundered the Ferryman's hut from the ground in its upward climb, and it crumbled down gradually, covering the old man and the youth.

The women cried out loudly and the temple rocked like a ship running unexpectedly aground. The two of them stumbled anxiously around the hut in the dawn. The door was locked and no one seemed to hear their knocking. They rapped harder and were quite surprised when at last the wood began to ring. The power of the lamp locked up inside the hut had actually transformed the interior to silver. But at length, it also began to change its form. The noble metal abandoned the fortuitous shapes of boards, beams, and posts, and extended itself into an elegant shrine of fine craftsmanship. An exquisite little temple now stood in the center of the larger one, or, if you will, an altar worthy of the temple.

The noble youth now clambered up a flight of stairs which ascended on the inside into the height. The man with the lamp lighted his way, and someone else in a short white robe holding a silver rudder seemed to be supporting the youth. This man was recognized at once as the Ferryman, who had previously occupied the transformed hut.

The beautiful Lily climbed up the outer steps which led from the temple to the altar, but she was still forced to keep her distance from her beloved. The old woman, whose hand had continued to wane as long as the lamp was concealed, cried out "Am I to become unhappier yet? With all these wonders, are there none to save my hand?"

Her husband pointed to the open door and said, "See, it's daybreak. Hurry up and bathe in the river.

"What kind of advice is that?" she cried. "I'll become completely black and disappear altogether. Haven't I already paid enough to cover my debt?

"Heed my words and go," said the old man; "all debts have been settled."

The old woman hurried off, and in that instant the light of the rising sun appeared on the border of the cupola. The old man stepped between the youth and the virgin and cried out in a loud voice "There are three who rule Earth: Wisdom, Appearance and Power. At the first word, the gold king stood up; at the second, the silver king; and at the third word, the bronze king slowly rose while the jumbled king suddenly crumpled up awkwardly.

Despite the moment's solemn note, whoever saw this sight could barely suppress his laughter, for the king neither sat nor reclined, nor was he leaning, but had sunk into a shapeless mass.

The Will-o'-the-wisps who had been busying themselves about him stepped to the side; though they seemed pale in the morning light, they were nonetheless well-fed again, and well-lit around the flames. They had deftly licked the golden veins of the colossal statue clean with their pointed tongues. The irregular empty spaces which this engendered remained intact for a while and the figure kept standing in its previous form. But when the last delicate little vein had been consumed, the image fell apart, unfortunately in precisely that place which remains whole when one sits. The joints, which should have bent, remained stiff. Whoever was unable to laugh had to avert his eyes; this half-breed object between form and clod was disgusting to look at.

The man with the lamp now led the handsome youth, who continued to stare into the void, from the altar to the bronze king. A sword in a bronze sheath lay at the feet of the mighty oligarch. The youth gird himself.

"The sword on the left, the right free!" shouted the powerful king. Then they turned to the silver king who pointed his scepter towards the youth. The prince gripped it with his left hand and the king said in a friendly voice "Tend the sheep!" As they approached the gold king, he pressed the garland of oak upon the youth's head with a gesture of patriarchal benediction and spoke: "Recognize the highest!"

During this procession, the old man had scrutinized the youth carefully. His chest swelled near the engirdled sword, his arms grew animated, and he stepped with a firmer foot. As he took the scepter in his hand, his strength seemed to relax and, by some inexpressible stimulus, to become more powerful; but as the oak garland adorned his locks, his facial features were revived, his eyes glistened with an indescribable spirit, and the first word his lips uttered was Lily!

"Darling Lily!" he cried as he ran after her up the silver stairs. She had been watching his course from the pinnacle of the altar.

"Dear Lily, were I a man who had everything, nothing would be more precious to me than the innocence and serene disposition which your heart reveals. O my friend," he continued, as he turned to the old man and looked at the three sacred statues. "Glorious and assured is our fathers' kingdom, but you've forgotten the fourth power which, still prior, more universally and more certainly rules the world: the power of love." Declaiming this, he flung his arms around the beauty's neck; she had thrown off her veil and her cheeks grew tinted with the prettiest undying rose.

To this, the smiling old man replied, "Love does not rule, it educates, and that is more."

Amidst all this pomp, jubilation and delight, no one had noticed that full daylight was streaming through the open portal, bringing in its train unexpected apparitions to greet the eyes of the company. A great room surrounded with columns formed a corridor at whose end could be seen a magnificent bridge with many archways spanning the river. On both sides, gloriously expansive colonnades had been erected for wanderers, many thousands of whom were already eagerly traveling back and forth. The wide lane in the middle was animated by herds and mules, riders and wagons, which flowed to and fro, like a stream unhindered on both sides. Everyone seemed to be overwhelmed with the freedom and majesty of this passage. Elated by their mutual love, the young king and his consort were especially captivated by the motion and vitality of this great people.

"Commemorate the Snake's good name," said the man with the lamp. "You owe her your lives, and the people owe her this bridge which only now unites the neighboring shores of these revitalized countries. Those shimmering and sparkling gems of the body she sacrificed are the foundation columns of this noble bridge; from them she raised herself, and she'll keep herself sound."

An illumination of this marvelous secret would have been desired had not the four pretty maidens stepped in through the entrance of the temple. Lily's entourage with the harp, the parasol and the taboret were recognized at once, but the fourth who was even prettier than the other three was unfamiliar. She teased them like a sister and they fluttered through the temple and ascended the silver steps.

"Will you believe me in the future, my dear?" said the man with the lamp to the lovely one. "May you and every creature prosper who bathes in the river this morning!"

The rejuvenated and beautiful old woman, who showed no marks of her former figure, embraced the man with the lamp in her youthful, exhilarated arms; and he returned her caresses with affection. "If I'm too old for you," he said with a smile, "you may choose another partner. From this day on, no marriage is binding which is not newly betrothed."

"Don't you realize that you've become younger yourself?" she replied.

"If I'm a gallant young man in your youthful eyes, then I'm happy; I accept your hand once more and will be happy to live with you beyond the next millennium."

The new queen welcomed her new maiden friend and descended with her and her playmates to the altar, while the king, in between the two men, peered out at the bridge and observed the crowd of people attentively.

His contentment did not last long. Looking out, he saw something which immediately displeased him. The great giant, who still seemed to be rubbing the sleep from his eyes, tumbled across the bridge, causing great disorder. He had risen up, typically drunken in his slumber, and thought he would bathe in a familiar river cove. Instead, he came onto solid ground and slipped on the broad flagstones of the bridge. Although he stepped between men and cattle in the most awkward manner, his presence affected everyone though no one realized it; but when the sun shone in his eyes and he raised his hands to rub them, the shadow of his monstrous fist flew behind him in such an awkward and violent manner through the crowd that people and animals collided in great masses, suffered injury, and risked the danger of being hurled into the river.

As he watched this outrage, the king automatically reached for his sword, but then reflected momentarily and looked calmly first at his scepter, then the lamp, and then the rudder of his companions. "I know what you're thinking," said the man with the lamp, "but we and our powers are helpless against this helpless creature. Stay calm! He's inflicted injury for the last time; his shadow is luckily turned away from us."

Meanwhile, the giant was coming closer and was amazed at what he saw with open eyes. His hands dropped to his sides and he did no more damage as he stepped into the corridor, staring with open mouth.

He walked straight to the temple gates when suddenly he was fixed to the floor in the middle of the courtyard. He stood there as a colossal and powerful statue of glittering ruby, and his shadow marked the hours which were inlaid upon the floor in a circle, not with numbers but rather with noble and significant images.

The king was overjoyed to see the giant's shadow beneficially aligned, and the queen was no less astounded by the strange sight which nearly covered up the view of the bridge from the temple as she ascended in glorious raiment from the altar, accompanied by her virgins.

Now that he stood still, the people began to crowd around the giant, and they goggled in wonder at his metamorphosis. Then the throng turned toward the temple, which they seemed to have only then perceived, and they advanced towards the door.

Instantly, the hawk swept high over the dome with the mirror and, catching a ray of sunlight, reflected it back to the group standing at the altar. The king, queen and their entourage in the dim vault of the temple appeared illuminated by a heavenly glory, and the people fell down in adoration. When they had all regained their senses and were standing once more, the king and his consort went down to the altar through the concealed halls to his palace, and the people scattered throughout the temple to satisfy their curiosity. They looked on in wonder and admiration at the three kings who stood erect, but were even more inquisitive to know what bulge could possibly be hidden behind the tapestry in the fourth niche, for whoever had done it, a well-intentioned modesty had draped an exquisite cloth over the king who had collapsed. No eye could penetrate it, and no hand dared to remove it.

The people would have never stopped gaping in admiration, and the pressing multitudes would have smothered themselves in the temple had their attention not been diverted again to the great room.

Unexpectedly, gold pieces seemed to fall from the sky, jangling down upon the marble tiles. The travelers closest to them scurried to hoard the coins, and the miracle was repeated several more times, first in one place, then another. It was not hard to discern the departing Will-o'-the-wisps, who were again amusing themselves as they squandered the gold taken from the limbs of the collapsed king in their own humorous style. The people ran around greedily for a while, pushing and shoving each other even after the gold pieces ceased to rain. Eventually, they slowly departed and went their way, and to this day the bridge abounds with wanderers and the temple is the most frequented on the entire earth.

# ⚭ The Counselor ⚭

In an Italian seaport, there once lived a merchant who had already in his youth distinguished himself by his industry and shrewdness. He was also a good navigator and had acquired great wealth by sailing to Alexandria to purchase and barter valuable goods that he then either sold in his native city or exported to Northern Europe. His skill grew by the year, especially so because his greatest pleasure was his own occupation, and he had no time left for expensive distractions.

He continued to apply himself diligently in this pursuit until his fiftieth year. The gregarious pleasures with which the orderly bourgeois spice their lives were little known to him; nor had the fairer sex, his countrywomen included, been able to arouse his attentions. He was too aware of their appetites for decoration and luxury, though he himself knew how to use these to his own advantage on occasion.

Little did he anticipate the change in disposition which came over him one day when his richly laden ship sailed into the harbor of his native city as a yearly festival in honor of the city's children was being celebrated. After church, boys and girls would appear in all kinds of costumes, sporting in processions and crowds through the city, then cavorting in games upon great clearings in the fields, where they played tricks and showed off their skill in friendly competitions to win little prizes.

At first our mariner enjoyed watching this celebration, but after a while of observing the children's exhilaration, their parents' delight, and so many people feasting on a joy of the moment in which they'd found the most pleasing of hopes, he was forced to reflect upon the conspicuousness of his own lonely situation. For the very first time, his empty house seemed dreadful to him, and in his thoughts he reproached himself.

"Oh what a wretch I am! Why have my eyes been opened so late in life? Why has it taken old age for me to recognize the only good things that make people happy? So much trouble! So many dangers! What did they bring me? My cellars are full of merchandise, my coffers full of precious metals, and my closets full of finery and jewels, but these goods can neither amuse me nor satisfy my soul. The more wares I amass, the more company they seem to demand. One jewel leads to another, one gold piece to another. They don't recognize me as the master of the house. Vehemently they call out to me, 'Go on, hurry up and bring back more of our kind!' Gold is only pleased with gold, and jewels with more jewels! They've been ordering me around in this way all my life, and only at a late age do I feel that there's no pleasure in it for me at all. Unfortunately, now that I'm getting on in years, I've begun to think and say to myself, 'You don't enjoy these treasures and no one will enjoy them after you! Have you ever adorned a lovely wife with them? Have you ever bestowed them upon a daughter? Have you ever put a son in the position of winning a good maiden's affection? Never! You and all your property! Neither you nor those who belong to you have really ever possessed anything, and what you've so painstakingly gathered together will be squandered away after your death by some stranger.'

"How different for those happy parents when they gather their children around the table to praise their skill and encourage them to noble deeds! What joy sparkled in their eyes! What hope seemed to emanate from all those gathered! Shall you yourself have no hope at all to embrace? Are you already senile? No! At this age, it's still not foolish to think of marriage. With all your wealth, you'll be able to win a fine wife and make her happy; and if there are to be children in your house, these late fruits will bring you the greatest pleasure instead of being a burden and a complication as they often are for those who receive them from heaven too early."

This inner dialogue brought him to a firm decision and he called over two of his shipmates to divulge his thoughts to them. They were accustomed to being ready and willing on all occasions, and this was no exception. They hurried in to the city to inquire after the whereabouts of the youngest and prettiest maiden, since this was the good their patron desired, so he should find and possess the best.

The merchant did not rest easy. He walked up and down, inquired, looked and listened, and soon found whom he was looking for in a young woman who deserved to be called the most beautiful in the whole city. She was about sixteen years old, well-educated and well-bred, and her figure and character were the most appealing and promising.

Following a short agreement, which assured the beauty a most favored portion during her husband's lifetime and after his death, the marriage was celebrated with great magnificence and merriment, and from that day on our merchant felt himself to be in true possession of his wealth, which he enjoyed for the first time. He now devoted himself with pleasure to arraying his lovely wife with the most beautiful and elegant material. The jewels sparkled on the breast and in the hair of his beloved in a way they never had inside the jewelry box, and the rings acquired an inestimable value from the hands which wore them.

And so he felt not only as wealthy but even wealthier than before, for his property seemed to increase as he shared and enjoyed it. In this way, the pair lived almost a year greatly satisfied, and the merchant seemed to have traded completely his love of an active and wandering life for the feelings of domestic bliss. But it's not easy to give up old habits; and though we can certainly veer from a direction taken early in life, we can never interrupt it completely.

And so when our merchant saw his other self setting sail or returning to the harbor, he too felt the impulse of his old passion again, and he even felt restless and discontented at home by his wife's side. This longing increased with time and was finally transformed into such a yearning that he felt extremely unhappy and finally became very sick.

"What shall become of you now?" he asked himself. "You've discovered how foolish it is to trade an old life style for a new one so late in life. How are we to drive the very things we've always sought after from our thoughts and our own bones? What's to become of me? Once I loved the water like a fish, and the free breeze like a bird. Now, I've confined myself in a house full of treasure with the flower of all riches, a beautiful young woman. I had hoped to win contentment and to savor my wealth but instead it seems that I've lost all of it because I can win nothing further. It's unjust to consider men foolish who restlessly acquire goods, for the activity is its own reward. For those who enjoy striving ceaselessly, acquired wealth is meaningless. Lack of occupation will make me miserable, lack of mobility will make me sick, and if I can't come to some other decision, I'll soon be near death. It's certainly a risky undertaking to distance oneself from a lovely young woman. Is it fair to set an alluring maiden free so that she may soon give herself up to her sensations and desires out of sheer boredom? Aren't there already these fellows in silk strutting back and forth in front of my windows? Aren't they already trying to draw my wife's attention to themselves in church and in the gardens? What will happen when I'm away? Am I supposed to think that my wife will be rescued by some miracle? No, at her age and with her sensibility it would be ridiculous to hope that she would be able to maintain the joy of our love. If you leave, when you return you'll find that you've lost your wife's affection, her devotion, and with it the honor of your house."

The reflections and doubts with which he tormented himself for a while extremely aggravated his state of mind. His wife, his relatives and friends were distressed by his condition without being able to discern the cause of his illness. He finally took counsel in himself again, and after a few considerations cried aloud, "You fool! You've become so sour guarding your wife that you'll die if this complaint continues, and then you'll have to leave her behind to someone else. Isn't it at least more sensible and better to save your life when you're in danger, though it means losing precisely that treasure which women prize highest. Even a husband's presence cannot always prevent the loss of this treasure, and many men must patiently endure the absence of what they can't cling to. Shouldn't you have the courage to be free of such a good when your very life depends on this decision?"

He took heart in these words, charged his shipmates to load a ship for departure and to prepare to set sail with the first favorable wind. Then he explained himself in the following way to his wife.

"Don't be surprised if my movements around the house suggest that I'm preparing to travel. Don't grieve, I must admit to you that I'm planning a voyage. My love for you is the same and it will certainly remain so as long as I live. I know the virtue of happiness by your side, and would feel its purity even more were I not forced to reproach myself silently for being idle and irresponsible. My old inclination has reawakened and my old habit beckons me. Allow me to visit the market of Alexandria again. I'm eager to obtain the finest material and the noblest gems for you there. I'm leaving you in possession of all my property and my fortune. Help yourself to it as you wish and enjoy yourself with your parents and relatives. The period of my absence will also pass, and it will enhance the joy of reuniting with you."

His obliging wife tenderly reproached him with tears in her eyes. She assured him that without his presence not a single hour would pass happily for her, and she implored him to think of her often, as she could not hold or confine him.

After he had discussed various business and household concerns with her, he paused briefly and said, "There is still a matter weighing heavily upon my heart, which you must allow me to express frankly. I beg you most sincerely not to misunderstand what I say, but to recognize the extent of my love in this anxiety of mine."

"I can guess its nature," replied the beauty. "You're worried for my sake, just like men who think our sex is weak. You've known me to be young and happy and now you think that I'll become foolish and easily misled in your absence. I won't scold you for thinking this way since it's so typical of you men—but knowing my heart as I do, I can only assure you that nothing can influence me in the least. No possible impression can affect me so deeply as to lead me from the path of love and devotion I've been following. Don't worry, you'll find your wife just as tender and faithful when you return as you found her on the evening when you returned to her arms after a short absence."

"I trust you when you say that these are your sentiments," replied the husband, "and I beg you to be constant in them. But let's look ahead and suppose the most extreme situation occurred. You know how much the eyes of our young men are drawn to your pretty and alluring figure. When I'm not here, they'll trouble themselves all the more for your sake. They'll try every trick to get close to you and to win your favor. Your husband's image, like his presence now, will not always be able to drive them from your door and your heart. You're a noble and good child, but the promptings of nature are powerful and not to be underestimated; they're constantly at odds with our reason, and they are usually victorious. Don't interrupt me. No matter how devoted you keep your thoughts, you'll feel the longing which draws man to woman and woman to man. I may be the object of your desires for awhile, but who knows what circumstances and opportunities will present themselves. Another may reap the reality of what the imagination had meant for me. Don't be impatient, hear me out!

"In the event that you cannot remain without a man's company —a possibility which you deny and which I by no means wish to expedite—and can no longer bear to be without the joys of love, promise me only that you will not choose one of these frivolous youths to take my place. However pleasing their appearance, they are more dangerous to a woman's honor than to her virtue. Ruled more by conceit than true passion, they trouble themselves for this and that woman's affection and find nothing more natural than to sacrifice one to the next. If you feel inclined to seek out a friend, search for one who really deserves the name; who knows how to exalt the joys of love modestly and with the discretion of secrecy."

His beautiful wife was no longer able to hold back her tears, which now fell copiously. Passionately embracing her husband, she cried out, "No matter what you think of me, nothing could be further from my mind than this crime which you consider unavoidable. Should such an idea ever enter my thoughts, may the earth open up and devour me, and tear me away from every hope of joy that our continued life together promises. Distance this mistrust from your heart and leave me with the pure hope of seeing you soon in my arms again."

After trying every way to console his wife, he set sail the next morning. His voyage was an auspicious one, and he soon reached Alexandria.

Meanwhile, his wife lived a withdrawn life with every luxury and comfort, undisturbed in her possession of a great fortune. With the exception of her parents and relatives, she made an effort to see no one else. Having found trustworthy servants to further transact her husband's business affairs, she occupied herself in the exquisite rooms of their mansion renewing the memory of her husband's presence every day.

Though she withdrew into a life of peacefulness, the young people of the city did not remain inactive, nor did they neglect to walk past her window frequently, trying to attract her attention in the evening with music and song. At first, the lonesome beauty found these exertions uncomfortable and burdensome. Yet, she soon grew accustomed to them, and during the long evenings she submitted. The serenades became a kind of pleasant conversation, and she didn't bother to wonder where they came from, nor did she hold back the many sighs meant for her absent husband.

She had hoped that her unknown admirers would grow weary, but their increased attempts seemed to become something permanent. She could now distinguish the ever-returning instruments, voices and melodies, and soon could no longer deny her curiosity to know who these strangers could be, especially the persistent ones. To while away the hours, she could certainly allow herself this pastime.

She now began occasionally to peek through the drapes and shutters to the street to watch the passers-by, especially to distinguish which men peered at her window the longest. They were most handsome, well-dressed young people, who nonetheless revealed in their manners, as well as in their entire appearance, as much triviality as conceit. They seemed to stand out more for the attention they paid to the lovely's house than for any kind of respect that they wanted to demonstrate.

"Truly," the lady said jokingly to herself every now and then, "my husband's idea was clever. In the conditions which allow me to take a lover, he excluded everyone who makes any effort on my behalf or who could possibly attract me. He knows quite well that prudence, modesty, and discretion are the qualities of a settled maturity which values understanding but which can't possibly excite our imagination or allure us. Those who besiege my house with their flattery certainly inspire no trust, and those whom I could trust do not seem desirable to me.

Assured in these thoughts, she allowed herself to indulge more and more in the pleasures of the music and in the figures of the youths passing by. Without noticing it, a restless longing began to grow in her breast which it was now too late to resist. The loneliness and indolence, the comfortable, good, and affluent life were the elements leading to an intemperate desire earlier than the good child had expected.

With quiet sighs, she now began to admire her husband's virtues, his worldly wisdom and knowledge of humanity, especially his knowledge of a woman's heart. "So it was possible that what I denied so strenuously could happen after all," she said to herself. "It was indeed necessary to be cautious and discerning in such circumstances. But what good are caution and prudence when fate seems to play unmercifully with such ill-defined desire? How can I choose someone I don't know? Am I to believe that one of my close acquaintances is the one?"

These and hundreds of similar thoughts only added to the confusion which possessed the beautiful woman. She tried in vain to distract herself. Every pleasing object stimulated her sensations, which in turn created pleasing pictures in her imagination.

In this state, she learned from one of her relatives, who was spreading town gossip, that a young scholar of jurisprudence, who had studied in Bologna, had just recently returned to his native town. One couldn't sing his praises highly enough. Besides an extraordinary intelligence, he demonstrated a sagacity and talent rarely possessed by young men, and considering his extremely charming appearance, he was quite modest. As a counselor, he'd won the trust of the citizens and the respect of the magistrates. He attended the courthouse daily to look after his professional duties.

The lovely wife listened to the description of so complete a man with a longing to know him better and with a silent wish to find in him the one to whom, according to her husband's dictates, she could entrust her heart. The moment she heard that he passed by her house every day, she became quite interested. She waited watchfully for the hour when the courthouse would convene. She was not unmoved when she finally saw him walk by. His handsome figure and his youth were particularly alluring to her, but she was troubled by his modesty.

She observed him secretly for several days and finally could no longer withstand the desire to attract his glances. She lavished attention on her appearance and stepped out onto the balcony. When she saw him coming down the street, her heart began to pound, but then it sank and she felt ashamed. He had walked by with measured footsteps as usual, focusing his eyes introspectively upon his meditations. He hadn't even noticed her.

She tried to get his attention for several days in a row, but to no avail. He always walked by at his normal pace without looking up or even glancing out of the corner of his eye; and the more she looked at him, the more he seemed to be the one she wanted. Her liking for him grew stronger every day, and since she did not resist it, it finally overpowered her. "How can it be!" she said to herself, "your noble and understanding husband knew the predicament you'd fall into when he left. His prediction that you'd be unable to live without a friend and favorite has come true. Why should you lament and despair just when luck reveals a youth so much to your liking and your husband's specifications, a young man with whom you can secretly savor the delights of love? You'd be a fool to let this chance slip away, a fool to refuse a love so powerful.

With these and many other thoughts, the beautiful woman attempted to support herself in her decision, and was tormented by doubt only for a short time. Finally, as so often happens when a passion we've withstood seizes us all of a sudden and so arouses our nature that we look back contemptuously on our worries and fears, caution and shame, relationships and commitments as just so many petty obstacles, she impulsively decided to send a young servant girl to the man she loved, and no matter what it would take, to possess him.

The maiden hurried off and found him sitting at a table with many friends. She promptly greeted him just as her mistress had instructed. The young counselor was not surprised by the message. In his youth, he had made the acquaintance of the merchant and he knew that the man was away at the moment. Though he only vaguely recalled having heard about his marriage, he supposed that the wife left behind in her husband's absence probably needed his counsel in some matter of importance. He replied to the girl most politely that he'd certainly visit her mistress as soon as they left the table. Words cannot express the beauty's delight when she heard that she soon would see and speak to her beloved. She hurried to put on her finest gown and had her rooms quickly and spotlessly cleaned. Orange petals and flowers were strewn throughout the house and the sofa was draped with the most exquisite tapestry. In this way, the short time before his appearance was spent in busy activity. It would have been unbearable otherwise.

With what agitated poise did she approach him when he finally arrived! What discomposure when she sat down on the sofa and invited him to sit on the taboret next to her! In the presence of this man she had longed for, she became speechless. He, too, was quiet and sat modestly in front of her. She finally pulled herself together and said to him, not without some apprehension and uneasiness:

"Sir, you've only recently returned to your home town and are already known to be a talented and trustworthy man. I, too, entrust you with an important and unusual affair which, when I consider it properly, belongs more to the concerns of the father confessor than to those of the jurist. A year ago, I married a wealthy and honorable man who gave me the greatest attention as long as we were living together. I would not be lamenting this man had not a restless desire to travel and trade torn him from my embrace not long ago.

"As an understanding and upright man, he sensed the injustice he did me by leaving. Realizing that a young wife could not be guarded like jewels and pearls, he knew that she was more like a garden of pretty fruit which would spoil were she selfishly kept under lock and key for several years. Therefore, he spoke with me sincerely before leaving. He assured me that I'd be unable to live without a friend. Not only did he grant me permission, but he urged and entreated me to promise that I'd freely follow my heart's desire without hesitating."

She paused momentarily, but a promising look from the young man gave her enough courage to continue her confession.

"My husband added one condition to his otherwise so considerate permission. He advised me to exercise the utmost discretion and expressly ordered me to select only a friend who is constant, trustworthy, prudent and discreet. Spare me from having to say the rest, sir. Spare me the awkwardness of confessing how much you captivate me and how much I see my hopes and wishes in your trust."

After a short silence, the charming young man replied carefully: "I'm greatly obliged to you for this trust. You honor me and make me happy. I truly hope I can convince you that you haven't appealed to someone unworthy of you. First, let me reply to you as a scholar of jurisprudence. As such, I must admit to you that I admire your husband who so clearly felt and examined his injustice, for it's certain that someone who abandons a young wife to visit faraway regions of the world is to be seen as one who has renounced his claim to any other property and has obviously forsaken all rights to it. Since the first person to come along may seize whatever has become free, it seems only natural and fitting that a young woman in such a circumstance should again bestow her affections on a friend whom she deems pleasing and trustworthy.

"However, in the event that the husband himself acknowledges his misdeed, and expressly allows the wife left behind to pursue that which he cannot prohibit, there remains absolutely no doubt, especially since no injustice can be committed against someone who has explicitly affirmed his willingness to submit to it.

"But if you choose me to be your servant," the young man continued with an entirely different look and the most spirited expression, as he took his pretty friend by the hand, "then you grant me a happiness which I'd never have conceived possible until now. Be assured," he exclaimed as he kissed her hand, "that you couldn't have found a servant more loyal, gentle, true, and discreet."

How consoled she felt after this declaration, nor did she shy from exhibiting to him the most passionate tenderness. She squeezed his hands, moved closer to him, and lay her head upon his shoulder. They did not remain in this position for long before the young man gently attempted to distance himself. Sadly, he began to speak: "What more unusual a situation could a man be in? I'm forced to distance myself from you and to exert the utmost restraint at the very moment when I should be giving myself up to the sweetest sensations. At the moment, I may not dedicate myself to the happiness which awaits me in your arms. Oh, I hope that this delay won't rob me of my most beautiful hopes!"

Anxiously, the lovely woman asked the reason for such an unusual pronouncement.

"As I approached the completion of my studies in Bologna," he replied, "and was struggling very hard to make myself adept in my future profession, I fell into a terrible sickness which threatened to shatter my powers of mind and body, if not to destroy my life entirely. In my dire need and under the severest pains, I vowed to the Mother of God that if she would allow me to recover, I would fast strictly for an entire year and would refrain from all pleasures—no matter what they might be. I've fulfilled this vow most faithfully for ten months now, and considering the great gift I received, the months have not been long ones. It wasn't hard for me to go without those familiar goods which I'd taken for granted. But the two months remaining will seem like eternity to us now—only after they've passed may I enjoy that happiness which exceeds all conception. Please don't let this time make you weary. Don't draw back the hand which you so freely extended to me."

The beauty, not particularly satisfied with this explanation, was nonetheless encouraged when her friend, after deliberating momentarily, continued to speak. "Dare I suggest to you the means which would deliver me earlier from my vow? Were I to find someone who could keep the vow as strictly and certainly as I, and who would share half of the burden for the remaining time, I would be free that much sooner, and then there would be no obstacles to our desires. Would you be willing, my sweet friend, to further our happiness by clearing away part of the hindrance? I can only transfer a part of my vow to the most trustworthy person. It is strict. I'm allowed only bread and water twice a day, and may spend only a few hours each night on a hard bench; and regardless of my many business concerns, I must say an immense number of prayers. If I can't avoid attending a banquet, as in the case today, I must nonetheless abide by my commitment and try all the more to resist the enticement of every sweet morsel offered to me. If you'd follow these rules for a single month, you'd possess a friend with that much more enjoyment, for you would have earned him yourself through such a praiseworthy undertaking."

The beautiful lady was not pleased to learn of the hindrances opposing the object of her inclinations. Yet, the young man's presence served to increase her love for him so much that no test seemed to be too severe if it would assure her the possession of such a valuable good. She thus spoke these most pleasing words to him: "My sweet friend! The miracle of your convalescence is itself so exceptional and laudable that I make it my joy and obligation to share this vow which you're required to fulfill. I'm pleased to give you such certain proof of my affection. I will follow your counsel most precisely, and nothing will sway me from the path until you release me yourself."

After the young man had described every particular of the conditions, according to which she could save him half of his vow, he departed with the assurance that he'd visit her again soon to inquire about her perseverance in following the resolution. So she had to let him go. He left without squeezing her hand, without a kiss, and with barely a meaningful glance.

Fortunately for her, the unusual commitment gave her much with which to occupy herself, for she had a lot to do if she were to alter her way of life so completely. First of all, she cleared away the pretty petals and flowers which had been strewn for his visit. Then, in place of the plushly cushioned sofa, she substituted a hard bench where she lay down at night, barely sustained on bread and water for the first time in her life. The next day, she was busy cutting and stitching shirts, a specified number of which she'd promised to complete for a poorhouse and hospital. During these new and uncomfortable occupations she always strengthened her imagination with her sweet friend's image and with the hope of future happiness. With these thoughts, her scanty sustenance seemed to give her heart nourishment.

A week passed in this way and at its close, her rosy cheeks began to pale. Clothes that usually fit her well were now too large, and her limbs, otherwise so lively and nimble, had become weak and languid when her friend appeared again. His visit gave her new strength and life. He admonished her to remain true to her commitment, encouraged her with his own example, and intimated the hope ahead of undisturbed delight. He stayed only a short time and promised to return again soon.

The charitable work was resumed with a new sense of cheerfulness, and the strict diet was in no way neglected. But unfortunately, a terrible illness could not have consumed her more. Her friend, who visited her again at the end of the week, looked at her with the greatest sympathy and strengthened her with the thought that the first half of the test was already behind her.

The unaccustomed fasting, prayer, and work now became more

burdensome by the day, and the excessive asceticism seemed to have completely unsettled the healthy condition of a body so used to rest and plentiful nourishment. The lovely woman could no longer support herself on two feet and was obliged, despite the warm season, to wrap herself in two and three layers of clothing to preserve as much as possible her nearly vanished body heat. No, she was no longer capable of standing up and was finally compelled to keep to her bench.

What reflections she must have had about her condition! How often this peculiar circumstance hovered silently before her soul; and how painful it was for her to suffer ten days straight without her friend appearing—he who had required these extreme sacrifices. Yet, these gloomy hours were the preparation for her complete recovery. Yes, it was certain. As soon as her friend appeared and sat next to her bench on the same sofa where he'd first heard her declarations, and implored her amiably, even tenderly, to withstand the short time remaining, she interrupted him with a smile and said, "My precious friend, I don't need persuasion anymore, and I'll endure my vow these few days with patience and with the conviction that you imposed it upon me for my own good. I'm too weak at the moment to express my heartfelt thanks to you. You allowed me to be true to myself. You have given me to myself and I realize that I owe my entire existence to you from now on.

"Truly! my husband was understanding and prudent, and he knew the heart of woman. He was fair enough not to reproach her for the affections which arose in her breast because they were his fault. Indeed, he was generous enough to put the demands of nature before his own rights. But you, dear sir, are reasonable and good. You've allowed me to feel that there's something in us besides inclination, and that it is just as important that we're capable of renouncing every accustomed pleasure and can even dismiss our most passionate desires. You initiated me in this school through struggle and hope, but neither are necessary once we've finally become acquainted with the good and powerful Self abiding so calmly and peacefully within us, which continually makes its presence known through gentle reminders until it finally becomes the Lord of the house. Farewell! You'll soon have the pleasure of seeing your friend again. I hope that you have the same

effect on your fellow citizens that you've had on me. Don't just extri-
cate them from the complications attending to matters of property,
but show them by gentle guidance that the power of virtue is hidden
like a seed in every human being. Your reward will be the people's
respect for you, and more than the most pre-eminent politician or the
greatest hero, you'll deserve the title: Father of the nation."

# ☾ *The New Melusina* ☽

ESTEEMED Gentlemen! Knowing that you do not particularly savor opening addresses and introductions, I want to assure you without further delay that I hope this time especially to meet your behest. Certainly I've already imparted many true stories to great and unanimous satisfaction, but today I have one to tell which, I must say, far excels all the preceeding; and though it happened several years ago, the memory of it still disturbs me; yes, it even offers hope of a perfected development. You'd look hard to find one like this.

First of all, I must confess that I haven't always managed my life with an eye to security in the time ahead, or even the next day. I was not a good proprietor in my youth and often found myself in all sorts of embarrassing situations. One day I decided to take a trip, which was to procure me a good profit, but I cut my slice a little too thick. Having set out with an express-coach, and then pursuing my course with a regular stagecoach, I was finally obliged to continue the rest on foot.

As a vital youth, I'd always had the habit, once I'd arrived at an inn, of searching out the proprietess, or even the cook, to flatter, the usual outcome of which would be a reduced bill.

One evening as I stepped in the coach house of a small town and proceeded in my customary manner, a handsome double-seated coach harnessed with four horses clattered up to the door behind me. I turned around to see a woman by herself, without chambermaid or servants. Immediately, I hurried to open the door for her, asking her whether I could be of any assistance. A gorgeous figure stepped from the carriage, and her charming face, upon closer inspection, was adorned with a slight trace of melancholy. Again, I asked whether there was anything I could do for her. "Oh yes!" she said, "if you would carefully pick up the little chest sitting on the seat and carry it upstairs; but I beg you to hold it quite upright and not shake it." I carefully took the little chest, she closed the coach door, and together we walked up the stairs where she informed the porter that she would be staying the night.

We were now alone in the room. She called me to put the little chest on the table against the wall, and when I noticed her gestures indicating that she wished to be alone, I took my leave by respectfully but passionately kissing her hand.

"Order dinner for the two of us," she said in reply, and you can imagine the delight with which I heeded her request. In my excitement, I was barely able to look over my shoulder at the proprietor, the proprietess, and porter. Impatiently, I waited for this moment to be with her again. Dinner was served, we sat down across from each other, and for the first time in quite a while, I had a good meal at the same time that I enjoyed such a delicious view; yes, it seemed to me that she became prettier by the minute.

Her conversation was pleasant, but she avoided pursuing any topic related to love and affection. When the table was cleared, I lingered. I sought every pretext to get closer to her, but in vain. She held me at arm's length with a certain dignity which I could not resist; yes, against my will I had to leave her after a fairly short time.

After a most sleepless and unsettling night filled with dreams, I woke up early and inquired whether she had ordered her horses. "No," I heard, and strolled into the garden when I spotted her standing dressed in the window. I bounded up the stairs to see her. As she seemed so beautiful to me, appearing even more gorgeous than the night before, I was excited to caprice, roguishness, and daring. Rushing up to her, I embraced her in my arms. "Irresistible, angelic creature," I cried, "forgive me, but I can't help myself!" With unbelievable agility, she escaped my embrace before I could even plant a single kiss on her cheek.

"Restrain yourself from such sudden outbursts of passionate affection if you don't want to throw away a happiness which is close at hand, but can only be possessed after a few tests."

"Ask of me what you will, angelic spirit!" I exclaimed, "but don't lead me into despair."

Smiling, she replied, "If you would dedicate yourself to my service, then listen to my conditions! I've come here to visit a friend with whom I intend to spend a few days. In the meantime, I wish my coach and this little chest to be further transported. Will you assume the responsibility? You've nothing more to do than lift the chest carefully in and out of the carriage. When it's in the coach, sit next to it and watch over it attentively. Should you come to an inn, it's to be placed on a table in a special room where you may neither enter, reside, nor sleep. You are to lock the room each time with a special key which opens and shuts all locks, and which makes the lock resist any other key in the interim."

I looked at her and felt quite an odd sensation. I promised to do anything if I could hope to see her again soon, and if she would seal this hope with a kiss. She did, and from that moment on I was completely under her spell. I should order the horses to be harnessed, she said. We spoke about the path I was to take and the location where I was to wait for her. Then she pressed a purse of gold in my hand and I pressed my lips to her hand. She seemed to be moved by our separation, and I no longer knew what I had done nor what I should do.

After I'd ordered the horses to be brought, I found the chamber door locked. I tried my master key at once and it passed the test with flying colors. The door sprang open and I found the room empty. Only the little chest sat on the table where I had placed it.

The coach drove up; I carefully carried the little chest down the stairs and set it next to me. The proprietess asked, "And where's the lady?"

"She's gone into town," a child answered.

I bid adieu and drove off in triumph from the people whose door I'd entered the previous evening with dusty leggings. That I now ran this story back and forth in my mind leisurely, counted the gold, made all sorts of sketches, and occasionally cast furtive glances at the little chest, you can easily imagine. I now drove straight ahead, stopping off at numerous places but not resting until I'd arrived at one of the larger cities to which she'd summoned me. I followed her orders scrupulously, placed the little chest in a special room with a couple of unkindled lamps next to it, which she'd also ordered, locked the room, moved into my own, and made myself comfortable.

For a while, I was able to occupy myself with the memory of her, but very soon the time began to drag. I wasn't used to living without company; but soon enough I found some after my own taste at inn tables and in pubs. My money began to shrink on these occasions and one evening it disappeared altogether from my purse as I frivolously gave myself up to a game of passion. Arriving in my room, I was beside myself. Bereft of money and expecting a handsome bill in my guise as a rich man, uncertain if and when my beauty would show herself, I was greatly embarrassed. My yearning for her grew twofold, and I no longer believed that I could live without her and her money.

After dinner, which hadn't tasted good at all, since I was forced to savor it alone, I paced back and forth in my room, talked and cursed to myself, threw myself on the floor, tore the hair from my head, and generally disported myself in a thoroughly disgraceful manner. Suddenly I heard a rustling in the locked room next to me and shortly afterward a knocking at the well-secured door. I gathered myself together and grabbed the master key, but the folding door sprang open by itself, and in the shine of the burning lamps, my beauty advanced towards me. I threw myself at her feet, kissed her dress, her hands, and she lifted me up from the floor. I didn't dare embrace her, let alone look her in the face; but I confessed to her openly and regretted my mistake. "It's forgiven," she said. "You've merely postponed your happiness and mine. You must now ride further in the world before we see each other again. Here is some more gold, which will be sufficient if you economize. If wine and games have embarrassed you this time, then guard yourself against wine and women and let me look forward to a happy reunion."

She stepped back across the doorway, the leaves shut together; I knocked, I pleaded, but she gave no indication that I was heard. When I received the bill the following morning, the waiter smiled and said, "So now we know why you've locked your doors in such a skillful and incomprehensible way that no master key can open them. We suspected that you had lots of money and valuables, but now we've seen the treasure walking down the stairs, and it seemed in every way worth guarding."

I said nothing in reply, paid my bill and stepped into the carriage with the little chest. I rode off further into the world with the firmest resolution of heeding my secretive friend's warning in the future. Yet I'd barely arrived in a large city when I became familiar with charming women from whom I could in no way escape. They seemed to attach a high price to their favors, for although they always held me at a certain distance, they invited me to one treat after another, and since I only sought to further their pleasures, I never thought twice about my purse but paid and spent with ease as the situation warranted. How great was my amazement and delight when I realized after a few weeks that the fullness of the purse had yet to be diminished. It was just as round and swollen as it had been at the outset. I wanted to be more certain about this admirable property, so I sat down to count and note the sum exactly. Then I carried on with my companions just as lustily as before. Nor was there a want of journeys by land and sea, nor lack of song and dance and other pleasures. Little attention was now required, however, to see that the purse was indeed shrinking. It was just as if my damned counting had robbed its capacity of being beyond accountability. Meanwhile, the life of glee was in full swing and I couldn't turn back, yet I was nearly at the end of my means. I cursed my situation, reproached my sweetheart who'd led me into such temptation, and blamed everything on her for not coming to me. Angrily, I renounced all my obligations to her and made up my mind to open the little chest—to see whether it might contain some assistance. It wasn't heavy enough to contain money, but there could have been jewels inside and these would have been quite welcome. I ruminated over carrying out the plan, but delayed until nighttime to perform the operation silently, and hurried off to a banquet which had just been announced. The festivities then recommenced and we were considerably elevated by wine and trumpet blare when I was suddenly dealt the bad hand: my dearest love's old friend, returning from a journey, entered unexpectedly and sat down at her side. Without great formality, he attempted to take his old liberties and this resulted in indignation, sharp words, and argument. We finally came to blows and I was dragged home, half-dead with numerous wounds.

When the surgeon had bandaged me and left, it was already late at night and my attendant had fallen asleep. The door of the side room opened and my secretive friend walked in and sat down beside me on the bed. She asked how I felt; I didn't answer because I was weak and ill-humored. She began to speak with great sympathy and rubbed my temples with a special balsam so that I felt quickly and decisively rejuvenated. In fact, I felt so rejuvenated that I lost my temper and scolded her. I blamed her vehemently for all my bad luck, for the passion she'd excited in me, for her appearance and disappearance, for the boredom, and for the yearning I had to endure. I became more and more fervent, as if I'd contracted a fever, and I finally swore to her that if she wouldn't be mine, wouldn't belong to me this time, wouldn't join me, then I had no desire to live any longer; this said, I demanded a definite answer. When she clumsily hesitated to explain I completely flew off the handle and ripped the twice- and thrice-bound bandage from the wound with the decided intention of bleeding to death. How astounded I was to find my wounds healed, my body clean and glowing, and her in my arms.

We were now the happiest pair in the world. We pleaded with one another for mutual forgiveness and didn't really know why. She now promised to travel further with me, and we were soon side by side in the carriage, the little chest across from us in the place of the third party. Not once had I ever discussed this little chest with her, nor did it now strike me to mention it though it stared us both in the face, and we were silently agreed to watch over it as the situation demanded. I continued to carry it in and out of the coach as before, and busied with locking the coach doors.

As long as there was still money in the purse, I'd always spent liberally. When the cash on hand came to an end, I called it to her attention. "That's easily provided," she said, and pointed to a pair of little bags strapped to the side of the coach overhead, which I'd certainly noticed earlier but had never needed. She reached into one of them and withdrew a couple gold pieces and then pulled a few silver coins from the other, disclosing to me the possibility of pursuing any extravagance we desired. So we traveled from city to city, country to country, happy by ourselves and with others, and the thought that she'd ever leave me again never entered my mind—all the less since she'd recently begun to reveal a new bounty, which only added to our joy and love. But unfortunately one morning I couldn't find her anymore. Since the stopover was dreary without her, I set off on the road again with my little chest. I tried the virtue of both the sidebags and found them still trustworthy.

The trip continued pleasantly without incident. Since I expected the peculiar occurrences to have a perfectly natural outcome, I never thought twice about my adventure. But now something happened which not only astonished me, but made me anxious and afraid. Accustomed to traveling restlessly day and night, I often rode in darkness, and if the lanterns happened to flicker out, it was often dark inside the coach. Once I fell asleep on such a dark night and when I woke up, I saw the glow of a light on the coach ceiling. Looking closely, I realized that it emanated from the little chest which seemed to have a split in it. It was as if summertime were bursting through the hot, dry atmosphere. My thoughts about jewels being excited again, I suspected that the chest contained a carbuncle, and I wished to be more certain. I sat up as straight as possible to keep my eye level with the fissure. How astonished I was as I peered into a room well-lit with lamps and furnished with much taste and splendor. Yes, it was just as if I were looking down through the opening of a vault into a king's chamber. What's more, I could see only part of the room. The rest was concealed from view. A fireplace appeared to be burning and next to it stood an armchair. I held my breath and continued to peep. A woman walked from the other side of the room with a book in her hands. I recognized her at once as my sweetheart, though her likeness was fashioned in the tiniest measurements. The lovely one sat down in the armchair by the fireplace to read, setting the poker with little firetongs in an upright position. As she moved, I could see clearly that this most charming little creature was expecting a child. I found it necessary, however, to shift my uncomfortable position somewhat, and when I looked again to make sure that I hadn't been dreaming, the light had disappeared and I was looking into empty darkness.

You can imagine how shocked I was. Though a thousand thoughts about this discovery raced through my brain, I really couldn't think at all and gradually fell asleep. When I woke up, I believed that I'd dreamt the whole thing, but I felt somewhat estranged from my sweetheart. As I carried the little chest all the more cautiously, I didn't know whether I desired or dreaded her reappearance in fully human proportions.

Shortly thereafter, my beauty stepped into the evening wearing a white dress, and as twilight shadows swept across the room, she appeared taller than I was accustomed to seeing her. I remembered having heard that gnomes and nixies assume a longer appearance at night fall. She flew into my arms as she always did, but I couldn't hold her tightly against me with a genuine feeling of happiness.

"Dearest," she said, "I'm unfortunately aware of your feelings, to which I'm very sensitive. You've seen me in the interim. You were instructed of the situation in which I find myself between our visits. So your luck has been interrupted, and so has mine. In fact, it seems to have been shattered completely. I must leave you and I don't know if I'll ever see you again." Her presence and the loveliness with which she spoke instantly wiped away every memory of the face which had been hovering before me like a mere dream. I embraced her warmly, convinced her of my passion, assured her of my innocence, and told her how the discovery had been an accident. In a word, I carried on to such an extent that she seemed moved and tried to console me.

"Ask yourself honestly," she said, "whether this discovery has damaged your love, whether you can forget that I live by your side in two forms, and whether the diminution of my being will also diminish your affections."

I looked at her. She was prettier than ever. I thought to myself: is it really such a great misfortune to have a wife who's a gnome every now and then, and can be carried around in a little chest? Wouldn't it be a lot worse if she were a giant and stuck her husband in a box? My cheerfulness returned. I wouldn't have let her leave for anything in the world. "My dear," I replied, "let's stay together and live as before. Could the two of us find anything finer? Comfort yourself as you will, and I promise you that I'll carry the chest even more discreetly. How could the loveliest thing I've ever seen affect me adversely? How happy all lovers would be if they could possess such a miniature likeness! It was only a likeness after all, a sleight of hand. You test and tease me, but you'll see how constant I can be."

"It's more serious than you think," said the beauty. "Nonetheless, I'm really quite pleased that you take it so lightly, for that can have the happiest consequences for the both of us. I want to trust you, and to that end will do everything I possibly can. However, you must promise never to reproach me about this discovery. Moreover, I beg you to guard yourself more than ever against wine and anger."

I promised to do all she asked. I'd have promised to do even more but she herself changed the subject, and so everything went on as before. We had no reason to leave our present stopover. The city was large, the society diverse, and the season occasioned many country and garden festivities.

My lover was quite appreciated at such entertaining events. Yes, she was desired by men and women alike. Her good-hearted and ingratiating manner, combined with a certain nobility, won her everyone's love and respect. She also played the lute splendidly and sang in accompaniment. Her talent was the crowning touch of every social evening.

Now I must confess that I've never been fond of music. In fact, it has much more of an unpleasant effect on me. My lovely wife soon noticed this, and therefore never attempted to humor me in this way when we were by ourselves; but she compensated for this in social settings where she usually found many admirers.

And now—why should I deny it—our last discussion hadn't been sufficient to quell this thing in me, despite my best intentions. My sensibility, on the contrary, had become oddly attuned without my becoming fully conscious of the fact. Then one evening, my bad temper broke lose in a large gathering, and the largest portion of this loss was served to me.

When I think back on it now, I loved my beauty much less after that unfortunate discovery, and now I became jealous of her, something that had never happened before. At the dinner table, where we sat diagonally at a fair distance from one another, I found myself comfortably between my neighbors: two ladies who had appeared most delightful to me for some time. Amid jokes and talk of love, the wine flowed freely. Across the table, a couple of music-lovers had overpowered my lover and were inciting and leading the company in song, individually and in unison. This put me in a terrible mood. They seemed pushy, the singing angered me, and when even I was asked to sing a solo, I became truly incensed, drained my cup and set it down very ungently.

The charm of my two neighbors subdued me again at once, but anger is an evil thing once it's been set into motion. Secretly, it continued to simmer, even though everything should have inclined me to a joyful and forebearing disposition. On the contrary, I became even more malicious when the lute was given to my beauty to accompany her song to the admiration of all the rest. A general silence was unfortunately requested. I wasn't even supposed to talk anymore. The notes made my teeth ache. Was it any wonder then that the smallest spark should finally detonate the mine?

The moment the singer completed her song amidst the greatest applause, she looked over at me with a truly loving glance. Unfortunately, the glance didn't sink in. She had noticed that I'd tossed down a goblet of wine and had filled it again. Pointing at me with her right index finger, she warned me tenderly. "Remember that it's wine," she said in a voice loud enough for only me to hear.

"Water's for nixies," I bellowed.

Turning to my two neighbors, she said, "Ladies, crown the goblet with all your graces that it not be empty too often."

Turning to me, one of them hissed in my ear, "Surely, you won't let yourself be outdone."

"What's the dwarf want?" I hollered, disdainfully overbearing as I tipped over the goblet.

"Much has been spilled here," cried my wonderful beauty, plucking a string as if to draw the company's attention to herself and away from this disruption. She succeeded in this, especially when she stood up to play more comfortably, and continued her prelude.

When I saw the red wine flowing across the tablecloth, I came back to my senses. I recognized my great mistake, and felt profoundly heartbroken. For the first time, the music spoke to me. The first stanza she sang was a friendly song of farewell to the company, as there was still a feeling of intimacy. But with the following stanza, the group dispersed in every direction. Everyone felt single, separated out, and no one believed himself to be present any longer. But what can I say about this last stanza? It was directed solely to me. The voice of wounded love was bidding farewell to anger and arrogance.

I solemnly led her home, expecting nothing good in store for me.

Yet, when we reached our room, she became extremely friendly and gracious—even mischievous—and she made me the happiest of men.

The next morning, I said quite hopefully and full of love, "You've so often sung at the bidding of polite society; for example, that touching song of adieu last night. Now for my sake, sing a pretty and cheerful welcoming to this morning hour, that we may feel like we did when we first met."

"I cannot do that, my friend," she replied seriously. "The song last night was about our separation. That must now commence without delay. I can only tell you that your insult to our promise and oath has the direst consequences for both of us. You frivolously tossed away a great happiness, and now I must also renounce my most heartfelt wishes."

When I pleaded at this point, urging her to explain herself more precisely, she replied, "I can regretfully do that all too well, since my stay with you has ended. Understand, then, what I'd have preferred to hide from you until the last moment. The form I was in when you happened to see me in the chest is the natural form I was born with. I'm from the lineage of King Eckwald, the mighty Prince of Gnomes, of whom true history has recounted so much. Our people are just as active and industrious as in olden times, and are therefore easy to govern. You mustn't imagine that the gnomes have lagged behind in their work. On the contrary, the hurled spear which pursues an enemy, invisible and binding chains, impenetrable shields and the like are their works of greatest notoriety. But now they're occupied mainly with things of comfort and adornment, and in these they surpass all other peoples of the earth. You'd be overwhelmed were you to tour our workplaces and warehouses. Everything would be fine had a certain circumstance not entered the picture for the nation as a whole, and especially for the royal family."

When she paused momentarily, I urged her to further disclose this fascinating secret. She immediately complied.

"It's well known," she began, "that when God had created the world and the earth was dry and the mountains were mighty and majestic, that God, I say, at once created the gnomes before any other creature, so that reasoning beings might look on in awe and admiration into clefts and passageways at His wonder within the earth. It's further known that this little generation rose up later and tried to assume mastery of the earth. Therefore, God created the dragons to drive the gnomes back into the mountains. The dragons liked to nest in the great caves and crevices, and were accustomed to dwell there. They also spit fire and created other havoc, inflicting great peril and misery upon the little gnomes, who not knowing what to do, submissively and urgently turned to God the Lord in prayer to destroy this filthy generation of dragons. If now it was not part of God's wisdom to destroy His creatures, He nonetheless took the great affliction of the gnomes to heart. At once, He created the giants to combat the dragons, and if not wipe them out, at least to diminish their number.

"But when the giants had more or less finished off the dragons, they were filled with daring and conceit, and they also began to perpetrate wickedness against the good gnomes, who again turned to the Lord in their distress. God in His strength created the knights to battle the giants and dragons, and live in harmony with the gnomes. So from this side, the work of creation was completed. Ever since then, giants and dragons, knights and gnomes have always existed in association with one another. So you can see, my friend, that we're of the world's oldest generation—certainly an honor, but not without its disadvantages.

"Since nothing in the world lasts forever, but everything once great must become small and wane, we too have been declining and growing smaller since the world was created. This is especially true of the royal family, who by virtue of their pure blood are the most heavily subjected to this fate. As a way out, our wise men many years ago thought up the idea of sending a princess from the royal family into the country from time to time to marry an honorable knight, that the generation of gnomes might be rejuvenated and saved from total ruin."

As my beauty wholeheartedly spoke these words, I looked at her skeptically because it seemed as if she were playing me for a fool. I had no further doubts abut her charming origins, but that she mistook me for a knight made me somewhat mistrustful, since I know myself all too well to have believed that God had created ancestors of mine first thing.

I hid my amazement and doubt and asked her amiably, "But tell me, my dear child, how did you come to this large and noble figure? I know few women whose glorious features can compare to yours."

"That you shall learn," replied my beauty. "From time immemorial, the gnome kings had advised that this exceptional step be postponed as long as possible—which I consider quite natural and proper. They might have delayed even longer had my younger brother not been so tiny that when in his diapers the nurses actually misplaced him, and no one knows where he went. In response to this incident, unheard of in the annals of the gnome kingdom, the wise men assembled and at once resolved to send me in search of a husband."

"Resolved!" I cried. "That's all well and good; resolutions can be declared and minds made up, but how did your wise men give a gnome such a divine form?"

"Our forefathers also provided for this," she said. "In the royal treasury lay a monstrously large golden ring. I refer to it as it looked to me as a child, for it is the same ring that I'm wearing on my finger here. We then set to the task ahead. I was instructed by everyone of all that awaited me, and was taught what to do and endure.

"An exquisite palace, modeled after my parents' favorite summer chalet, was constructed with a main edifice, side wings, and everything else you could desire. It stood at the entrance of a great cleft in the rocks, which it embellished in the finest style. On the appointed day, the royal court moved in, along with my parents and myself. The army paraded and twenty-four priests carried the marvelous ring on a bier, and not without some difficulty. It was placed upon the threshold of the edifice inside the doorway. Many ceremonies took place, and after a heartfelt goodbye, I set to work. I stepped inside, touched the ring with my hand and instantly began to grow noticeably in size. In a few moments, I'd attained my present stature, and then I placed the ring on my finger. Instantly, the windows, doors, and gates shut closed. The side wings were drawn into the main structure and instead of a palace, a little chest stood next to me, which I picked up at once and carried with me—not without a pleasant feeling of being big and strong, and yet still a gnome compared to trees and mountains, streams and acres of land. And yet, I was still a giant compared to grass and plants, especially compared to ants, with whom we gnomes are not always in good standing, and are therefore often plagued by them.

"How I fared in my pilgrimage before I met you is a story in itself. Let me just say that I tested many but no one seemed worthy to revitalize and immortalize the lordly lineage of Eckwald until you appeared."

As I heard these tales, my head nodded every now and then without my actually shaking it. I asked various questions to which I received no remarkable answers. On the contrary, I learned to my dismay that after what had happened between us, she'd have to return to her parents. She hoped to return to me, but it was now imperative for her to present herself at court if all was not to be lost for both of us. The purse would soon be empty, and who knew what would happen?

When I heard that we'd soon be out of money, I questioned no further but shrugged my shoulders and grew silent. She seemed to understand me.

We packed our bags and boarded the coach. The little chest sat across from us. I still couldn't envision it as a palace. We continued in this way from station to station. Money for the journey and gratuities were promptly and lavishly paid from the right and left sidebags. We finally reached a mountainous region. Having barely stepped from the carriage, my beauty led the way and I followed her with the little chest. She led me up a fairly steep path to a narrow grassland. Through it flowed a clear brook, quietly meandering in serpentine twists. There she showed me a knoll, called me to set the chest down and said, "Farewell! You'll have no trouble finding the way back. Think of me, I hope to see you again."

In this moment, it was as if I couldn't let her go. She'd just come into her finer days, or if you will, finer hours. To be alone with such a beautiful creature on a green meadow between grass and flowers, encircled by mountains and surrounded by rushing water, what heart could have remained untouched? I wanted to take her by the hand, to embrace her, but she pushed me back and warned me kindly of the great danger that awaited if I didn't leave immediately.

"Is there no possibility then," I cried, "that I can stay with you, that you could hold me by your side?" I accompanied these words with such a pitiful behavior and tone that she seemed moved, and after a moment's consideration admitted that a continuation of our relationship would not be entirely impossible. Who could have been happier than I? My forwardness, which became ever more lively, finally compelled her to express her plan. She told me that if I'd be willing to become as small as I'd seen her, then I could stay with her in her house, in her kingdom and with her family. This suggestion did not entirely please me, but at that moment I couldn't tear myself away from her; so having become familiar with the miraculous some time ago, and already inclined to rash decisions, I agreed to the proposal and told her that she could do whatever she wished with me.

I was to stretch out the little finger of my right hand at once. She touched it with her own, pulled the golden ring from her finger with her left hand and brushed it up against mine. This had scarcely happened before I felt an excruciating pain on my finger. The ring contracted together and tormented me horribly. I screamed violently and grabbed at random for my beauty, but she'd disappeared. Words cannot express the state I was in at that moment. All I can say is that very soon I found myself in miniature next to my beloved in a forest of grass blades. The joy of seeing her again after such a short but so unusual a separation exceeds all conception. I flung my arms around her neck, she answered my caresses, and the little pair was just as happy as the larger pair had been.

With some difficulty, we now climbed up a hill, for the meadow had become an impenetrable forest for us. We finally reached a clearing, and I was dazzled to see a huge symmetrical mass, which I was soon forced to recognize as the little chest—in the same state as it was when I had set it down.

"Go on, my friend, and knock with the ring. You'll see wonders," said my sweetheart. I stepped up to it and no sooner had I knocked when I experienced the greatest wonder. Two side wings opened out, and at the same time various pieces fell here and there like shavings and scales. Suddenly, doors, windows, columned passages and everything that belongs to a palace in full regalia came into view.

Whoever has seen one of Röntgen's handcrafted desks, which at a single tug sends springs and latches into motion, with lectern, pens, letters, and money compartments folding out thereafter, would be able to imagine how that palace unfolded. My sweetheart now ushered me into the main room, where I immediately recognized the fireplace which I'd previously seen from above and the armchair where she sat. And when I looked up, I really believed that I saw the niche in the cupula through which I'd peered. I'll spare you the description of the rest. It's enough to say that everything was spacious, exquisite, and tasteful. I'd barely recovered from my bewilderment when I perceived military music in the distance. My better half jumped for joy and announced the arrival of her father, the king. We stepped through the doorway and saw a regal procession coming from a large cleft in the rocks. Soldiers, servants, dynastic officials, and a distinguished royal household followed in order. Finally, a golden multitude could be seen, and in its midst, the king. When they'd all assembled before the palace, the king and his entourage stepped forward. His affectionate daughter ran up to him, gracefully pulling me with her, and as I found myself standing before him, I realized for the first time that I had the most handsome stature in this tiny world. Together we proceeded to the palace where the king, in a well-rehearsed speech before the presence of his entire court, expressed his surprise to find us here. He deigned to welcome me as his son-in-law and appointed the wedding ceremony to take place the following day.

How horrified I suddenly became when I heard talk of marriage, for I feared that even more than music itself, which had always seemed the most despicable thing on earth. Those who make music, I was in the habit of saying, at least they imagine themselves to harmonize and be in tune with one another; for when they've honked loud and long enough and rent our eardrums with every kind of dissonance, they stubbornly and resolutely believe that they've hit the right note and that one instrument corresponds to the next. The conductor himself lives in this happy madness. Thus, they proceed to pierce our ears joyfully. This is not at all the case with regard to marriage. For although it's only a duet, and one should think that two voices, even two instruments, could be somewhat attuned to each other, this is seldom true. When the husband sings a note, the wife sings one higher, and then the husband sings higher still. So the note rises from the chamber to the chorale ever further so that the wind instruments themselves can't follow it. Since harmonic music still grates on my nerves, my complete inability to tolerate disharmony can hardly be held against me.

I cannot, nor do I desire to relate all the festivities that transpired during that day. The costly meals, the exquisite wine—none of it tasted good to me. I brooded and pondered on what I should do. But there wasn't much to ponder. I decided that, come night, I'd slip away and hide somewhere. Fortunately, I was able to reach a stone crevice into which I squeezed myself, hiding as best I could. My first endeavor was to take the unlucky ring off my finger, but I was completely unable to do this. In fact, it felt more constraining the moment I thought of removing it, and I suffered quite a pain which immediately abated as soon as I gave up the effort.

I woke up early in the morning—for my little body had slept quite well—and wanted to look around further when something like rain began falling around me. It fell abundantly through the grass, leaves, and flowers like sand and grit, and I was horrified to find everything around me in animation, and then an endless army of ants trampled down upon me. No sooner had they perceived me when they attacked from all sides. Though I defended myself courageously enough, they closed in so thickly, biting and pinching me, that I was relieved to hear them calling me to surrender. I gave up at once and an ant of handsome stature approached me politely—yes, even respectfully—and commended himself to my favor. I discovered that the ants had become allies of my father-in-law, and that he'd called upon them to retrieve me. So here was little me in the hands of those even smaller. I envisioned the wedding and must still thank God that my father-in-law wasn't enraged or that my lovely had become cross with me.

I've nothing to say about the ceremony; suffice it to say, we were married. However happily ever after it went with us, there were still those lonely hours when I drifted into contemplation, and I was faced with something I'd never encountered before; what and how, you'll soon discover.

Everything around me was fully proportioned to my present size and needs. The glasses and goblets were scaled for a small drinker, and you could even say that they were more appropriate in size than they are with us. The tiny bites tasted delicious to my little palate, a kiss from wife's little lips was ever so exciting, and I can't lie, the novelty of it all was highly enjoyable. Nonetheless, I'd unfortunately not forgotten my former state. I felt a measure of my previous size within me and it made me restless and unhappy. For the first time, I now grasped what the philosophers might have meant about the ideal, which is supposed to plague humanity so. I had an ideal of myself, and often appeared to myself as a giant in my dreams, so that finally my wife, the ring, this gnome figure and so many other constraints made me so miserable that I began to think earnestly about my freedom.

Because I was convinced that the entire magic was hidden in the ring, I decided to file it off. I borrowed several files from the court jeweler. Luckily, I was left-handed and had never done anything right in my life. I persevered in my work, though it wasn't easy. As thin as the ring appeared, it had become thicker in its smaller scale. I spent all my free time unnoticed in this endeavor and was clever enough to step out the door before I'd filed through the metal. I did it. The golden band suddenly sprang violently from my finger and I shot up to the heights with such a velocity that I thought I had hit the sky, or in any case that I had crashed through the dome of our summer palace and destroyed the whole chalet in my new-found clumsiness.

So there I stood again, obviously larger, but also all the more stupid and clumsy, or so it seemed. When I came out of my daze and my wits recovered, I saw the strongbox next to me. It seemed fairly heavy when I lifted it up and carried it along the footpath to the station where I ordered the horses harnessed at once and drove off. Along the way, I tried the side bags. In place of the money which seemed to have been spent, I found a little key which belonged to the strongbox. Inside I found a fitting substitute. As long as that held out, the coach served my purposes. Afterwards, this was sold to bring me back by express coach. Finally, I disposed of the strongbox, for I doubted that it would replenish itself; and that's how I finally returned, although by a considerable detour, to the cook's hearth where you first met me.

# ⚆ The Good Women ⚆

HENRIETTA had been strolling up and down for some time with Armidoro in the garden, where the Summer Club tended to gather. They were cultivating the liveliest appetites for one another, and were often the first to arrive. In this pure and cultured society, they nurtured the most pleasing hopes for a lasting, future relationship.

Having seen Amelia walking toward the summer house in the distance, the spirited Henrietta ran to greet her friend. Amelia had just seated herself at the vestibule table, which was covered with journals, newspapers, and current magazines.

Amelia spent many evenings here reading, undistracted by the company's comings and goings, the clinking gambling chips, and the usually loud conversation of the players in the clubhouse. She spoke little, except when she asserted a contrary opinion. Henrietta, on the other hand, who was not sparing with her words, always seemed content, and had compliments fresh at her fingertips.

A friend of the editor, who we'll call Sinclair, approached the two friends. "Have you something new?" Henrietta called out to him.

"You'll never guess," replied Sinclair as he pulled out his portfolio. "And even if I tell you that I have the copper plates for this year's Ladies' Calendar, you'll still never guess their themes; of course, if I further reveal that the ladies are presented in twelve types. . . ."

"So!" remarked Henrietta, cutting him short, "it seems that you want to credit us with no perceptivity. And if I'm not mistaken, you're joking with me because you know I'm fond of charades and riddles, and love to guess what people are thinking. So, twelve women characters or situations, or allusions, or whatever else might contribute to the dignity of our sex."

Sinclair kept silent and smiled, Amelia glanced at him with the fine, sarcastic manner which suited her so well, and said, "If I read his expression correctly, he has something which is less than favorable to us. Men are oh so knowledgeable when they've found something which they think disparages us."

SINCLAIR "You're suddenly so solemn, Amelia. I sense a threat of bitterness. I dare not show you my little folios."

HENRIETTA "Oh, out with them!"

SINCLAIR "They're caricatures."

HENRIETTA "My very favorite!"

SINCLAIR "Etchings of vile women."

HENRIETTA "Even better. That category certainly doesn't apply to us; we can't take our disagreeable sisters seriously, in pictures or society."

SINCLAIR "Shall I?"

HENRIETTA "Go ahead!"

She grabbed the briefcase from his hand, withdrew the etchings, spread six folios out on the table, quickly skimmed them, and sorted through them as if she were reading cards.

"Superb!" she exclaimed, "Now that I call life-like! This one here, holding the pinch of snuff to her nose, looks just like Mme. S., whom we'll see here tonight. This one with the cat almost looks like my great aunt. The woman with the ball of thread reminds me of our old milliner. Every one of these ugly figures corresponds to some sort of archetype, the men as well. I've seen a stoop-shouldered pedant just like that somewhere, and the figure holding the yarn reminds me of someone, too. These little etchings are really funny, and they're etched quite handsomely.

"How can you possibly recognize specific similarities here?" Amelia quietly remarked, as she shot a cold look at the etchings and at once turned away. "Ugliness resembles the Ugly, beauty resembles the Beautiful; our spirit turns away from one and is drawn to the other."

SINCLAIR "But a preoccupation with ugliness, rather than with beauty, is an advantage to fantasy and wit. Much can be made from ugliness; from beauty, nothing."

"But it elevates us. Ugliness is degrading," said Armidoro, who had been standing at the window and listening from a distance. Without approaching the table, he walked off into the adjoining room.

All club societies have their epochs. The group's common interests and the good rapport of the individuals among themselves have their ups and downs. Our club has hit a high point this summer. Most of the members are refined, temperate, and tolerant people, who mutually appreciate each other's merits and leave what is unworthy alone. Everyone finds amusement, and the level of the general conversation invites participation.

At this moment, Seyton and his wife arrived. He was a man who had traveled a lot, first on business, then through political dealings. He was agreeable company and was especially welcome in wider circles as an ombre player. His wife, a lovely, good, and faithful consort, enjoyed her husband's complete trust. She felt fortunate that he happily allowed her to indulge her lively sensuality, for she couldn't live without an intimate, and only amusements and distractions could give her the resilience for domestic virtue.

We treat our readers as strangers, as club guests whom we spontaneously enjoy acquainting with our society. The poet should reveal his characters by their actions; but in recording conversations, we may abbreviate to guide our reader quickly through the exposition by a general account.

Seyton stepped over to the table and looked at the etchings. "We're in the midst of a dispute for and against caricature," said Henrietta. "Which side are you on? I'm in favor of them. Don't you think that every caricature has something irresistibly alluring?"

AMELIA "Isn't all slanderous gossip spoken behind a person's back enticing without being credible?"

HENRIETTA "Doesn't such an image make a lasting impression?"

AMELIA "That's precisely why I abhor them. Isn't the lasting impression of everything repulsive the very thing which haunts us throughout life, spoiling many a good meal and turning a good drink sour?"

HENRIETTA "Now, Seyton, what do you think?"

SEYTON "I suggest a compromise. Why should pictures be better than ourselves? Our spirit seems to have two sides which cannot exist without each other. Light and dark, good and evil, high and low, aristocratic and plebeian, and so many other polarities which, unevenly portioned, seem to be the ingredients of human nature. Why should I fault a painter who's painted an angel just as white, luminescent, and beautiful as it occurred to him, or who's painted a devil black, sinister, and ugly?"

AMELIA "There would be nothing to contradict what you say if the advocates of grotesquerie did not draw the properties of superior domains into their territory."

SEYTON. "I think you're quite right on that point. But the defenders of beautifying art also annex what can hardly belong to their province."

AMELIA "Nonetheless, I'll never forgive the caricaturist for so disgracefully misrepresenting portraits of eminent personalities. Contrary to my better judgment, I'm forced to think of the great Pitt as a pug-nosed ramrod, and the otherwise reputable Fox as a bloated swine."

HENRIETTA "That's what I said. All such distortions imprint themselves indelibly, and I must confess that I often enjoy conjuring up these phantom images and distorting them even more."

SINCLAIR "Ladies, let's interrupt the argument for a moment to consider these poor folios in front of us once more."

SEYTON "I see that the love of dogs has not been so generously represented."

AMELIA "I've no quarrel with that. These animals are especially repugnant."

SINCLAIR "First opposed to caricature, now dogs."

AMELIA "Why not? Aren't animals really just caricatures of human beings?"

SEYTON "Surely you must remember what a traveler recounted about the city of Grätz. He found it full of dogs and mute half-imbeciles. Isn't it possible that the habitual sight of barking, dumb animals could have some influence on the human race?"

SINCLAIR "A predilection for animals certainly diverts our passions and affections."

AMELIA "And if reason sometimes stands still, as the common German saying goes, it certainly stands still in the presence of dogs."

SINCLAIR "Fortunately, we have no one in the club who favors dogs like Mme. Seyton. She has a particular fondness for her whippet."

SEYTON "And this creature must be especially dear and important to me, her husband."

From a distance, Mme. Seyton raised a warning finger at her husband.

SEYTON "It proves what you stated earlier, Sinclair. Such creatures divert the affections. Dear child," he called to his wife, "may I tell our story? It's nothing to be ashamed of."

With a friendly nod, Mme. Seyton consented, and he began his story: "Both of us were in love and had decided to get married without really any forethought to domestic arrangements. At last, certain prospects were in sight. Unexpectedly, I was forced to travel again, and this threatened to detain me longer than I'd wished. When I departed, I left my whippet behind with her. It was always with me when I visited her and when I was away, but sometimes it stayed with her. Now that it belonged to her, it became a frisky companion and a sign of my return. At home, the dog was an object of amusement and seemed to search for me along the promenades on which we'd often strolled together. It would spring from the bushes as if to announce my arrival. My dear Meta fooled herself this way with the illusion of my presence until the time arrived when I'd hoped to return. The length of my absence suddenly threatened to double, however, and the poor creature lost heart and died."

MME. SEYTON "Quite sincerely, pleasantly, and reasonably recounted, my dear."

SEYTON "You're perfectly free to stop me whenever you'd like. So, the apartment seemed empty to my fiancée, and the strolls, uninteresting. The dog, who sat beside her when she wrote me letters, had become a necessity, just like the dog in that picture of the evangelist, and now the letters no longer flowed from her quill. She finally happened to find a young man who was willing to take the place of her four-legged companion at home and on walks. So, no matter how discreetly one might view it, the picture took on a dangerous hue."

MME. SEYTON "I must let you proceed as you see fit. A true story without exaggeration is seldom worth hearing."

SEYTON "A mutual friend, whom we treasured as a quiet but perceptive judge of human character, and a good counselor, had stayed behind; and he noticed the change in her during his occasional visits. He observed her behavior without comment and one day walked into the room with a whippet which looked just like the former one. The polite and sincere address, which he delivered along with his gift, the unexpected appearance of her favorite's likeness as if resurrected from the grave, and her sensitive heart's silent self-reproach at this sight all served to recall my image to life. The young representative properly distanced himself and the new favorite remained a constant companion. When I returned and took my dearest in my arms, I still mistook the creature for the former one and was not a little perplexed when it barked vehemently at me as though I were a stranger.

Modern dogs must not have the memories which dogs of antiquity had! I exclaimed. Ulysses was recognized by his dogs after many long years. This one's forgotten me after just a brief absence. And yet he's watched over your Penelope in his own peculiar fashion, she replied, promising to explain this ruse to me. This happened soon enough, and ever since then, our bond has been blessed with clear confidence."

MME. SEYTON "This story concludes the matter, I think. If it's all right with you, I'd like to stroll for an hour, for I'm sure that you'll want to sit down at the ombre table."

He nodded in agreement. She took her sweetheart by the arm and walked toward the door. "Dear child, take your dog with you," Seyton called after her. The entire company smiled, and he had to smile with them when he realized how appropriately this unintentional exclamation had suited the occasion. Accordingly everyone enjoyed a silent bit of mischievous glee.

SINCLAIR "You've spoken of a dog which brought good fortune to a relationship. Now I'll tell you about one which had a detrimental influence. I, too, loved a woman, traveled, and left her behind, with one difference: she didn't know that I wanted to possess her. At last, I returned. The many sights that I'd seen were still fresh in my memory; and like many returning travelers, I wanted to recount my experiences and delights to others, especially to her. I found her, however, quite actively involved with a dog. I don't know whether she did this out of some contrary spirit, which so often animates the finer sex, or whether this was just an unfortunate happenstance. But all she spoke of was the little beast's "adorable" qualities, good breeding, attachment, its amusing aspects; there I was, a man who'd been absorbing all the experiences of traveling throughout the world for years, and her only topic of conversation was this dog. I faltered, grew silent; I tried to recount so much else that I'd been devoting myself to in her absence, but I just didn't feel comfortable, and so I distanced myself. This was wrong of me, and I became even more uncomfortable. Anyway, from that time on, our association grew continually cooler, until it finally ceased to exist at all. In my heart, at all events, I attribute the real blame to that hound."

Stepping from the other room, Armidoro joined the group and said, "Were someone to gather stories portraying the influence these social creatures exert upon people, this would certainly make for a striking collection. In lieu of such an anthology, I'd like to tell you how a dog occasioned a tragic misadventure.

"Ferrand and Cardano, two noblemen, had had a friendly association since early youth. As pages at court and as officers in a regiment, they'd been through many adventures together and had deeply perceived each other's mettle. Cardano had luck with the ladies; Ferrand, with gambling. The former was whimsical with his talents and displayed bravado; the latter was deliberate and exercised restraint.

One day, when he'd just broken off a relationship with a woman, Cardano accidentally left his pretty little wolfhound behind with her. He acquired another, and he gave this one to another woman when the appropriate time had arrived to flee. From then on, he bid adieu to his sweethearts with a wolfhound. Ferrand was aware of this posturing, but never paid any particular attention to it.

Time separated the friends for many years, and it wasn't until after Ferrand had been married and was living at his estate that they saw each other again. Cardano spent some time at Ferrand's estate, then moved to the neighboring region, staying for over a year in this area where he had many friends and relatives.

One day, Ferrand happened to see a delightful little wolfhound at his wife's side. Being particularly fond of this breed, he picked it up, praised it, caressed it, and naturally asked his wife where she had acquired such a pretty dog. "From Cardano," she replied. He was seized at once by the remembrance of former times and incidents, and with the memory of Cardano's impudent emblem of inconstancy. The sense of the insulted husband overcame him. He fell into a rage, violently hurled the gentle animal from his caressing arms to the ground, and stormed off, leaving the yelping dog behind and his wife aghast. A duel with all sorts of nasty consequences, a silent agreement to separate, without actual divorce, and a shattered household conclude this story."

The story was not quite over when Eulalia joined the group. She was a woman who was desired wherever she went, and was one of the club's loveliest jewels. She was a cultivated spirit and a successful writer. The skillful artist's caricatures which ridiculed the fair sex were submitted to her, and she was invited to speak up on behalf of her good sisters.

"Now, I suppose an explanation of these ever-so-lovely portraits will adorn the Almanac!" Amelia said. "Some writer, perhaps, will be at no loss of wit to unravel our graphic artist's woven images into words."

As the editor's friend, Sinclair could neither dismiss the etchings nor deny that an explanation was needed here and there, for certainly no caricature could forego the explanation which alone would give it life. However much the artist troubles to illustrate a joke, he's out of his league all the same. Caricature without caption or explanation is, to a certain extent, silent; only language gives it substance.

AMELIA "Then put this little illustration here into words! It seems a woman has fallen asleep in an easy chair while writing. Another woman is standing next to her holding out a little bottle or receptacle and crying. What's that supposed to represent?"

SINCLAIR "Aha! The ladies seem to be neither well disposed toward these caricatures nor their explanation, and you want me to interpret? I'm told that the representation here is of a woman writer who tends to write at night. She insists that her chambermaid hold her ink bottle and stay standing in this position. Should the lady be overcome with sleep, the chambermaid is to remain standing, even if her function becomes useless, because the lady, upon awakening, wants to be able to pick up the thread of her thoughts and ideas, and the quill and ink with which to write them."

Arbon, a reflective artist who had accompanied Eulalia, contested the picture. "If you want to depict such a scene, you must proceed in a different way."

HENRIETTA "All right, let's recompose the picture from the start."

ARBON "First, let's look closely at the object. It's perfectly natural for someone to hold the ink bottle for a writer when there is no place to set it down. Brantome's grandmother held the ink bottle for the Queen of Navara when the Queen sat in her easy chair and wrote down the stories which we still enjoy reading. It's also fitting that a person would hold the ink bottle for someone writing in bed. All right, my lovely Henrietta, since you love to ask questions and guess so much, what should the artist do to depict such a scene?"

HENRIETTA "Remove the table and show the woman sleeping with nothing in her proximity to support an ink bottle."

ARBON "Good! I pictured her in an upholstered armchair, a Bergeres, if I'm not mistaken, next to a fireplace, so that we have a front view of her. She would have been writing on her lap, presumably, for we usually become uncomfortable ourselves when we cause someone else discomfort. The paper is falling from her lap and the quill is slipping out of her hand. A pretty girl stands next to her, holding the ink bottle and looking quite displeased."

SINCLAIR "I excuse the artist. He has left room in this one for the exegete."

ARBON "Who'll probably sharpen his wit on the two headless men hanging on the wall. This strikes me as a perfect example of the trap one falls into trying to combine art forms that don't belong together. If we weren't accustomed to captioned engravings, no etching would include them. I've nothing against graphic artists attempting to do humorous illustrations. I do think that they're difficult to accomplish, and the artist should create a form which explains itself. It's even permissible to have little bubbles with words coming from the character's mouth; but he should be his own commentator."

SINCLAIR "If you acknowledge a picture's humor, you'll have to admit that it entertains and stimulates only the informed, those who are familiar with the particular circumstances and situations depicted. Why shouldn't we appreciate the commentator who allows us to understand the humor?"

ARBON "I have nothing against explaining drawings which don't explain themselves, but the explanation should be as concise as possible. Jokes are only for the informed. Not everyone will understand a comical piece. We're barely able to decipher the humor we've inherited from distant times and places. That's why we append notes to

Rabelais and Johnson's *Hudibras*. What would you say to a writer who wrote a comical work to explain another comedy? Wit is already endangered by misunderstanding at the outset. It's bound to degenerate even further at second or third hand."

SINCLAIR "Instead of arguing, I really wish we could help our editor friend. He would want to hear the comments that these etchings have elicited."

ARMIDORO "So, these reproachable etchings are still engaging the group. Were they pleasing, they would have been set aside long ago."

AMELIA "I agree to that. Set them aside at once and be done with them. The editor must be persuaded not to use them. A dozen or more hideous, spiteful women in a Ladies' Calendar! Doesn't the man realize that he's about to undermine the whole project? What kind of lover, husband, or father would honor his beloved, his wife, or his daughter with such an almanac? She would be repelled the moment she opened it by images with which she has no affinity, nor should have."

ARMIDORO "I have a positive suggestion. These hideous portraits aren't the first to appear in fancy almanacs. Our gallant Chodowiecki has already etched monthly copperplates depicting unnatural, depraved, barbaric and distasteful scenes. How did he do it? He contrasted the despicable with the charming. He exhibited healthy nature in its slow growth, showing scenes of proper education, devoted perseverance, and the sensitive pursuit of excellence and beauty. Let's go beyond the editor's request and exhibit these contrasts. Since the graphic artist has chosen the shady side, let our author, or if I may voice my preference, our authoress, choose the side of light to bring about unity. Eulalia, I won't hesitate any longer. Take on the challenge of representing good women. Create some images in contrast to these copperplates here; instead of using your pen's magic to explain these images, annihilate them."

SINCLAIR "Do it Eulalia! Promise to do it as a favor to us, please!"

EULALIA "Authors promise all too easily because they hope to be capable of realizing their potential. My own experience has made me circumspect. But, if I should ever happen to have abundant leisure, I might contemplate such a proposition offered at such short notice. But whatever's to be said on our behalf must ultimately be said by a man, a young, fiery, loving man. If you want a favorable view, you need enthusiasm. Who has any enthusiasm for his own sex?"

ARMIDORO "Insight, justice, and tenderness in the exposition would be even more welcome."

SINCLAIR "From whom would you rather hear more about women than from the authoress who enraptured us ever so much with that exquisitely incomparable fairy tale of hers last night?"

EULALIA "That fairytale was not mine!"

SINCLAIR "Not from you?"

ARMIDORO "I can testify to that."

SINCLAIR "But from a young lady, then."

EULALIA "A girl friend."

SINCLAIR "So there are two Eulalias?"

EULALIA "Who knows how many more, and better."

ARMIDORO. "Would you tell us all what you confided to me? Every man will be surprised to hear just how such a fine creation came into being."

EULALIA "A young lady, whose acquaintance I learned to treasure while on a visit, happened to find herself in a particular predicament which would belabor us too long to explain here. A young man who had done a lot for her, and had finally offered his hand, won all her favors with it, took her quite off guard, and was granted all the privileges of a husband on a honeymoon. New events now necessitated the groom's speedy departure, and she found herself faced with the oh so joyous prospects of becoming a mother in some lonely country dwelling with not a few cares and anxieties. She was accustomed to writing me everyday to tell me the latest events. There were now no more incidents to frighten her—all she needed was patience; but in her letters, I noticed that past events and future prospects were all topsy-turvy in her agitated state. I decided to write her a sincere letter advising her of her duty to prepare healthy sustenance for herself and the creature whom she had introduced to life with such spirit. I encouraged her to get a hold on herself, and happened to send her a volume of fairy tales she'd requested. Her longing to free herself from misery and these fantastic productions came together in a curious way. Since she couldn't completely extricate herself from reflections upon her fate, she veiled, in fantastic forms, whatever had deceived her in the past and seemed frightening in the future. Everything that had happened to her—impulses, passions, mistakes, her winsomely anxious maternal feelings in such a delicate situation—embodied itself in incorporeal forms which paraded past in a colorful succession of odd apparitions. In this way, she spent the day and part of the night with pen in hand."

AMELIA "In which case, she would certainly have found it difficult to hold an ink bottle."

EULALIA "And that's how the most unusual sequence of letters I've ever received came into being. Everything was metaphorical, whimsical and fabulous. Since I no longer received any real news about her life, I sometimes feared for her mind. All of her circumstances, her delivery, her intimate love for her child, her joys, hopes, and motherly worries were occurrences of another world from which only her husband's appearance could free her. On the day of her wedding, she finished the fairy tale which you heard last night. It was almost entirely from her own pen, and its unique charm preserves the unusual and singular circumstances of its origin."

The group was at a loss for words to express their amazement at this story. Seyton, who'd relinquished his place at the ombre table, rejoined the company and inquired about the present topic of conversation. He was told briefly that it concerned a certain fairy tale which had arisen from the fantastic confessions of an ailing temperament.

"It's really too bad that diaries are outdated," he said. "They were very popular twenty years ago, and many a good youth believed that the daily entry of his humors was a real treasure. I recall a lovely person who soon discovered unhappiness in such a habit. A governess had accustomed her in her youth to write such a daily confession, and it finally became an almost indispensable concern. She did not neglect it as an adult, and continued the custom when she was married. She did not consider her diary to be especially secret and had no cause to. Sometimes she read passages to her girlfriends and sometimes to her husband. No one had a particular craving to read the whole thing.

"Time passed, and she, too, in turn possessed a lover. She wrote down the story of this new relationship just as conscientiously as she had recorded her other daily confessions. The entire course of this passion was accurately recorded from its first stirrings, through the growing affection, to the final need for her devotion, and it made curious reading matter for her husband who, without any suspicion, unintentionally happened to read an opened page of the journal as he walked past her desk one day. It seems that he took the time to flip back and forth through the pages. Finally, he set it down feeling rather hopeful, for he saw that there was still time to distance the threatening guest discreetly."

HENRIETTA "It was my friend's wish that our discussion concern good women, and now all of a sudden we're hearing about those who aren't really the best examples."

SEYTON "Why must it always be either good or evil! Must we not accept ourselves and others as nature has created us, or as we have better cultivated ourselves through education?"

ARMIDORO "I think it would be enjoyable and worthwhile if someone would record and collect narratives like the ones we've been listening to. It's good to be attentive to the slight details of a person's character, even if these give rise to no remarkable events. The novelist can't use them, for they aren't amusing and don't excite the spirit. Only those who enjoy the quiet contemplation of humanity will be receptive to them."

SINCLAIR "I agree. If we'd thought about such a laudable endeavor earlier, we could have assisted the editor of the Ladies' Calendar by collecting a dozen stories about good, if not excellent women to balance out these images of bad ladies."

AMELIA "I'd especially like to see someone compile the instances where a woman maintains the household, if she's not the very source of it. The more so since the artist here has represented a lavish and wasteful wife to the ridicule of our sex."

SEYTON "I have just such an example in mind, my dear Amelia."

AMELIA "Please tell it. But don't imitate the typically male style of beginning with flattery and ending with reproach."

SEYTON "This time, at least, I'm not worried about any evil spirit falsifying my intentions.

"A young countryman once rented a stately and well-furnished inn. Of the qualities that make a good innkeeper, he possessed leisure above all, and because taverns had been one of his enjoyments since his youth, he was happy to have chosen this enterprise so that he would need to spend the greater part of each day there. He was carefree without being dissolute, and he extended his good nature to all his guests, who soon became frequent visitors.

"He had married a young woman who was quiet and tolerant. She managed her responsibilities conscientiously, was devoted to her domestic concerns, and loved her husband; but silently, she had to reproach him for not being careful enough with money. She had a particular respect for ready cash, had a full appreciation of its value as well as the necessity of possessing and maintaining it. Without an innately cheerful disposition, she would have had a real aptitude for ruthless avarice. But a little avarice doesn't hurt a woman, however poorly extravagance becomes her. Generosity is a virtue which suits men, and attachment is a woman's virtue. Nature wanted it this way and our judgment must ever yield to nature.

"Margaret, which is the name I'll give to this concerned domestic spirit, was very dissatisfied with her husband when he left the payments, which he frequently received for bulk purchases of fodder, lying out on the table. He would simply stuff the money into a little box and dip into it without taking any account of his expenditures. She could see that even if he didn't squander it, such disorganization must be wasteful. The desire to direct him along a better path grew so great, and her dismay so spirited (seeing how much of the little bit which she could save was soon misspent and largely neglected), that she felt prompted to risk a daring attempt to open her husband's eyes to his own ways. She resolved to slip as much money out of his hands as she could, and she had a particular cunning to assist her in this. She'd noticed that he didn't count the money lying on the table a second time before putting it away.

"She rubbed tallow on the bottom of a candlestick and placed it in what would appear as an awkward position on the spot where the ducats of which she was so particularly fond had been left. She reeled in a bill and a couple of little coins next to it, and felt quite satisfied with her first catch. She repeated this operation more often. Since she had a good purpose, her conscience didn't bother her, and she quelled every doubt with the certainty that her expropriations could in no way be seen as theft because she hadn't taken the money with her hands. Her secret treasure gradually increased and became more plentiful as she held on tightly to all the ready cash that passed through her hands from the lodgers.

"She had been acting out her scheme for almost an entire year and had been carefully watching for any change in her husband's humor, without noticing a trace, until one day he fell into a highly irritable mood. She tried to coax from him the reason for his change in disposition and soon learned that he had fallen into a real quandary. After the last payment to his distributors, money should have been left over for the rent. Not only was it missing, but he hadn't even been able to pay off his suppliers completely. Since he calculated everything in his head and wrote down very little, he couldn't figure out where the mistake had been made.

"Margaret described to him his manner of collecting and spending money, his lack of attention, and she even attacked his good-hearted generosity. Naturally, the consequences of his business transactions provided him with little to defend himself. Margaret couldn't leave her husband in his embarrassment for long, the less so since it redounded to her credit to make him happy again. She astonished him on his birthday when, instead of her usual practical gift, she handed him a little box full of money. The various coins were specially wrapped and the contents were written on each roll very carefully in a simple script. How astounded the man was when he realized that he was looking at precisely the sum which he'd been missing, and which his wife assured him was his. She described to him in detail how and when she'd taken it, how much she'd taken, and what she'd been able to save through her own efforts.

"His annoyance turned into delight, and the consequence of it was that he let his wife take complete charge of the money affairs. From that day on, he pursued his business with even more enthusiasm but he never took another coin with his own hand. The woman supervised her office as cashier to her good credit. She took no counterfeit coins, and authority over the household was the outcome of her activity and diligence. After ten years, she was able to put her husband in a position to buy the inn and all that went with it."

SINCLAIR "So all this diligence, love, and devotion was really just to gain mastery. I'd certainly like to know just how justified it is to say that women are domineering."

AMELIA "Aha! Once again, we have the reproach hiding behind the compliment."

ARMIDORO "Tell us your thoughts about this, my dear Eulalia. I think I've noticed in your writings that you're not particularly worried about challenging this reproach."

EULALIA "In so far as it's a reproach, I'd wish that our sex refute the allegation through our own conduct; but insofar as we have the right to mastery, I wouldn't gladly relinquish it. We're fond of power only because we're human, for what else does mastery mean, in the sense which we've been using, than to be active in one's own way without any hindrance, to enjoy one's own existence to the utmost. This promotes arbitrariness in unrefined people, and furthers true freedom in the cultivated. Perhaps this aspiration seems more lively among women because nature, tradition, and social norms seem to restrict our rights and to favor the rights of men. Whatever men possess, we must obtain, and a person holds on tighter to what she's had to fight for than to what's been inherited."

SEYTON "And yet women can't complain any more. These days, they inherit as much or more than men, and I think that it's a lot more difficult now to become a complete man than to become a complete woman. The expression, 'and he shall rule over thee,' is the formula of a barbarous time which is long past. Men cannot fully develop themselves without according women equal rights. As long as women develop themselves, the scales are balanced; and if they're more capable of developing, experience shows that the scales will tip in their favor."

ARMIDORO "There's no question that in all civilized nations, women must gain superiority; for, in reciprocity, the man must become the more feminine, and this is a loss to him because his merit is not in moderate, but in disciplined strength. Yet, if a woman acquires something from a man, it's to her advantage, for if she can better her position with energy, the result is a being which could not be more perfect."

SEYTON "I haven't pondered the subject so deeply, but it seems generally well known that woman is the master and must be so. For that

reason, whenever I meet a woman, I'm attentive to her particular realm of mastery; that she rules somewhere, I take for granted."
AMELIA "And so you've proven your presupposition?"
SEYTON "Why not? Have the physicists and the others who've abandoned experience come up with any better results? In general, it seems that she who actively acquires and preserves rules the household; the beauty who is moderately and superficially educated rules the larger circles; and those educated in greater depth rule the smaller circles."
AMELIA "And so we've been divided into three classes."
SINCLAIR "Which are, I think, all quite honorable enough without exhausting the category of the feminine. For instance, there's still a fourth class regarding which we should probably say nothing so that no one can accuse us of changing our compliments to rebukes."
HENRIETTA "Are we to guess this fourth class?"
SINCLAIR "All right, our first three classes were power in the household, and in the greater and smaller circles."
HENRIETTA "What other area of our activity is there?"
SINCLAIR "There must be many, but I had the opposite of activity in mind."
HENRIETTA "Idleness! How can that be? Should an idle woman rule?"
SINCLAIR "Why not?"
HENRIETTA "But how?"
SINCLAIR "By refusing! Whoever persistently refuses either by force of character or as a matter of principle has a greater power than you might think."
AMELIA "I fear that we're about to fall into that common tone that one hears from men, especially when they pull out their flutes."
HENRIETTA "Leave him alone, Amelia. Nothing could be more harmless than such opinions. We always gain when we hear what another thinks. So, these aloof ones, what's their story?"
SINCLAIR "I must speak candidly here. There are a few of this class in our country, and none in France at all. This is because women in our country, as in neighboring countries, enjoy a certain measure of liberty. In countries where their freedom is restricted, where formal civility is overly scrupulous and public pleasure less frequent, such women can be found more often. In a neighboring country, someone

has even found a name for such a person. This is how the people, the observers of human nature, and yes, even doctors, classify such a woman."

HENRIETTA "I can't guess names, what is it?"

SINCLAIR "They're called, if it must be said, scoundrels (*schalke*).

HENRIETTA "That's peculiar enough."

SINCLAIR "There was a time when you read the fragments of the Swiss physiognomist with keen interest. Don't you remember reading something about scoundrels?"

HENRIETTA "Perhaps, but it didn't particularly strike me as noteworthy. I must have passed over the word without it registering as something particular."

SINCLAIR "Certainly, in common discourse, the word "scoundrel" refers to a person who delights maliciously in making another the butt of a practical joke; but in this context, the word refers to a woman who makes life sour for the person she depends on through aloofness, coldness, and denial—all of which she usually conceals behind the veil of illness. Every country has its own version. Numerous times when I had complimented the beauty of this or that woman, a native turned to me and said, 'But she's a scoundrel.' I've even heard that a doctor told a woman who'd been greatly abused by her chamber maid that, 'She's a scoundrel, and it would be difficult to help her.' "

Amelia stood up and left the room.

HENRIETTA "That seems a little unusual to me."

SINCLAIR "To me, too. That's why I wrote down the symptoms of this half-moralistic, half-physical malady in an essay entitled, "Scoundrels." Since I considered it part of other anthropological observations, I've kept it carefully hidden away."

HENRIETTA "You'll have to let us see it sometime. If you know a few good stories that can illustrate for us what exactly a scoundrel is, we'll add them to the collection of our newest novellas."

SINCLAIR "That's certainly a good idea, but I've failed in the intention which brought me here in the first place. I wanted to prompt someone in this lively group to write a text to these engravings, or to suggest someone who would do it. Instead, you've ridiculed and abused these folios, and now I have to leave without the explanation I came for. If I had only recorded on paper what we've spoken about this evening, I'd have an equivalent of what I was looking for."

ARMIDORO (stepping from the room to which he had repeatedly retired) "I can accommodate your wish. Our editor's concern is by no means foreign to me. I've quickly jotted down on this paper everything that was said, and I can flesh it out further. If Eulalia would grace the entirety with her charming spirit, at least our tone, if not the content, would absolve the women of the artist's uncouth insults."

HENRIETTA "I can't find fault with your active friendship, Armidoro, but I wish you hadn't written down the conversation. It presents a bad example. We all live together so cheerfully and with such trust, and there's nothing worse than to know that someone in a society listens attentively, writes everything down, and brings it to the public's attention, since everything gets published these days; especially since the conversation may be fragmentary and distorted."

Henrietta's fears were allayed with the promise that only the small anecdotes would meet the public eye in book form.

Eulalia could not be persuaded to edit the shorthand. She didn't want to be distracted from the fairy tale that was presently occupying her attention. The transcript remained in the hands of the men who, with the aid of their own memories, brought it to completion for the inspiration of all good women.

# Novelle

A TAUT autumn fog still cloaked the wide spaces of the palatial courtyard in the early morning when the lifting veil more or less revealed the entire hunting party moving haphazardly on horseback and on foot. The hurried activity of those closest could be easily recognized: they lengthened and shortened stirrups, parcelled out guns and ammunition, and straightened out the badger sacks, while the dogs on leashes threatened to drag away their restrainers. Here and there a horse bucked, driven by fiery nature and the spurs of the horseman who himself could not deny showing off a certain conceit here in the half light. All were waiting for the Prince, however, who, in parting from his young consort, lingered all too long.

Married only recently, they already had found happiness in harmonious dispositions. Both were of an active, spirited character, and they gladly shared each other's likings and aspirations. The Prince's father had lived to see and profit by the day when it appeared that all the subjects of the state should be equally creative and productive according to their abilities to earn first and enjoy afterwards.

Assembled at this time, the leading market, which could indeed be called a bazaar, testified to the success of this guiding principle. The previous day the Prince had led his wife on horseback through the myriad goods in stacks and had directed her attention to the prosperous exchange between the highlands and the plains; his districts' activity met at this very point, he informed her.

During this period, the Prince had consulted his councilors with almost exclusive reference to these pressing affairs, and worked continuously with the Finance Minister in particular. Nonetheless, the Master of the Chase maintained his authority. To his way of thinking, it was impossible during these auspicious autumn days to resist the temptation of a hunt, delayed once already, which would exhibit to the court and to the many newly arrived foreigners a unique and exceptional festivity.

The Princess stayed behind unwillingly. They'd resolved to force their way far into the mountain and to harass the peaceful inhabitants of the forest there with an unexpected war maneuver.

In parting, the husband did not neglect to suggest that she go on a short outing with his Uncle Friedrich. "I'll also leave our squire, Honorio, with you to take care of the court and the stables," he said. And with this he stepped down, gave the necessary instructions to a cultivated young man, and soon disappeared with the guests and retinue.

Waving with her handkerchief to her husband as he entered the courtyard below, the Princess now withdrew to the rear chambers of the palace. Here, there was a view of the mountain which looked even more majestic since the palace itself stood at a certain elevation above the river, and this afforded many interesting perspectives.

She found the excellent telescope just where it had been left the previous evening when, gazing out over bush, mountain, and treetop, they had discussed the ancestral castle ruins, which stood out remarkably in the evening's illumination; for at that time the greater amount of light and shadow conveyed the clearest idea of so stately a memorial to antiquity. And early this morning, the autumn hue of the various species of trees, which towered up between the masonry walls, unimpeded and undisturbed over the many years, presented a dazzling display through the looking glass. The captivating lady directed the scope somewhat lower, however, to a barren, rocky area which the hunting party would have to cross. She waited patiently and wasn't disappointed, for with the instrument's clarity and magnification power, her sparkling eyes clearly recognized the Prince and the Master of Horses. She couldn't resist waving her handkerchief once more, since it seemed almost (though not definitely) as if they had stopped a moment and looked back.

The Prince's Uncle Friedrich was then announced. He entered with his draftsman, who carried a large portfolio under his arm. "Dear niece," said the robust old gentleman, "we have some sketches of the family castle to show you. They're drawn from various angles to demonstrate how its reinforced structure has withstood time and the seasons, yet how its masonry is nonetheless giving way here and there and must collapse into utter ruin in particular places. Recently, we've done a lot to make this wilderness more accessible, for little more is necessary to astound and delight every pilgrim and visitor."

Pointing to the individual sketches, he spoke further. "Climbing up the ravine past the town walls, we reach the castle itself, here, where one of the most impregnable boulders of the entire mountain range looms up across the path. There's a tower at the top of it, though it's hard to tell just where nature ends and art and craft begin. In the distance, you can see walls bordering the sides and terraced baileys sloping down. That's not really a faithful description, though. Actually, the forest encloses this ancient summit; there's been no sound of an ax here in a hundred and fifty years, and the mightiest trunks have grown up everywhere. As you force your way through to the walls, you're confronted by trunks and roots of smooth maples, rough oaks, and slender spruces. We have to worm our way around these and plot our footpath judiciously. See how exquisitely our maestro has expressed this characteristic on paper, and how distinctly the various types of trunks and roots are entwined between the masonry walls, and how the thick branches are twisted through the fissures. It's a wilderness like no other, a capriciously singular location where the old traces of long-vanished human mastery can be seen vying most seriously with an eternally vital and flourishing nature."

Displaying another folio, he continued: "What do you think of the castle yard here? It's been completely inaccessible since the old bastille collapsed years ago. We attempted to approach it from the side, broke through walls, blasted vaults, and cleared out a snug but hidden passageway. It needed no clearing inside, for nature has leveled the rock's peak to a flat surface. However, here and there immense trees have still had the fortune and opportunity to strike roots. They've grown up gradually, but they haven't relented and now their branches extend into the galleries where the knights paced back and forth, and even through the doors and windows into the domed chambers. Yet, we've no desire to dislodge them. They're the masters now, and may prevail so. When we cleared away the deep beds of leaves, we discovered that the remarkable place had become smoothly flattened. Perhaps there's nothing quite like it to be seen in the entire world.

"But besides all this, what's even more remarkable—and you'd have to be there to see it yourself—is that a maple has taken root in the steps which lead to the main tower. It has grown so stout that it's now quite difficult to climb over it to get up to the battlement's unrestricted view. But it's pleasant to linger in the shadows here too, for this is the tree which towers marvelously high in the open air over the whole.

"We're indebted, then, to the worthy artist who has so laudably persuaded us of these things with his various pictures that it's as if we were present among them. He's devoted the finest hours of the day and the season to this, and has been exploring around these objects for weeks. We've arranged a comfortable little dwelling in this corner for him and also for the watchman whom we sent to him. My dear, you wouldn't believe what a beautiful view and vantage point he's provided looking over the landscape, courtyard, and walls. Now that he's outlined everything so neatly in detail, he'll be able to add the crowning touches at his leisure down here. We could decorate our garden room with these sketches, and then no one would let their eyes roam over the symmetrical flowerbeds, porticos, and shady colannades without wishing to be up there as well, in true contemplation of the old and the new, the petrified, unyielding, and indestructible; and the flourishing, supple, and invincible."

Honorio entered and announced that the horses were harnessed. Turning to the uncle, the Princess said, "Let's ride up there so that I may see the reality of what you've shown me here in sketches. Since I've been here, I've heard about this project, but only now do my own eyes long to see what seemed impossible in accounts of it, and fantastic in these reproductions."

"Not yet, my dear," replied the old Prince. "What you see here is what it can and will become. There are still many obstacles blocking the way. Art must first become consummate if it's not to shame itself before nature."

"Then let's at least ride up in that direction, if it's only to the foot of it; I've a great desire to see the world's vastness today."

"As you wish, by all means," replied the old Prince.

"But let's ride through town over the great market place," she continued. "A countless crowd of booths there has taken on the appearance of a small camp or city. It's as if the manifest needs and pursuits of every family in the surrounding territory had been revealed and assembled at this central point. The attentive observer sees everything people produce and need here. For a moment, you even imagine that money's not necessary, that every transaction can be settled by barter; and it is so, after all. Since the Prince provided the occasion yesterday for these perspectives of mine, it pleases me to think that here, where mountains border the plains, both articulate what they need and desire quite clearly. The mountain dweller knows how to transform forest timber into hundreds of shapes and can fit iron to a diversity of purposes; and the plainsman meets him with so many kinds of products that you can hardly discern their material or identify their function."

"I know that my nephew devotes the greatest attention to this, since it's especially important at this time of year to receive more than one gives. The entire state budget, just like the economy of the smallest household, is summed up in this goal. But forgive me, my dear, I never like to ride through markets and fairs. A person's every step is hindered and halted, and then that awful disaster ignites my imagination as though it were branded into my eyes when I saw just such a row of goods and merchandise go up in flames. I'd barely. . ."

"Let's not spoil these fine hours," interrupted the Princess, for the worthy man had already frightened her several times before with a lengthy description of that calamity. Weary from his travels one evening, he had gone to bed in one of the finest inns off the market place, which was crowded by a leading fair, and he had been dreadfully awakened during the night when screams and flames convulsed his room.

The Princess hurried to mount her favorite horse, and instead of riding to the rear gate and up the hill, she led her escort to the front gate and down. He yielded, grudgingly, for who would not have gladly ridden by her side; who would not have gladly followed her? Even Honorio was willing to forgo the otherwise desirable hunt to be exclusively at her service.

As foreseen, they could only ride at a slow pace through the market, but the beautiful and charming Princess enhanced every step with a clever remark. "Necessity wants to test our patience, so I'm reconsidering yesterday's instruction." And in fact, the entire mass of people crowded the riders so tightly that they could only proceed very slowly. The people were delighted to see the young lady, and the many smiling faces exhibited unmistakable pleasure to see that the country's first lady was also the prettiest and most graceful.

Mingling amongst themselves were mountain dwellers who made their home amidst precipices, spruces and pines; flatlanders from hills, pastures and meadows; merchants of the small town, and everyone else who had gathered here. The Princess, after quietly scanning the crowd, remarked to her escort how all these people wherever they came from used more fabric than necessary for their clothing, more cloth and linen, more ribbon for braiding. "Isn't it as if they couldn't flaunt themselves enough?"

"We'll certainly allow them that," the Uncle replied. "When people can devote themselves to their surplus, they're content, and most content when they embellish and decorate themselves by means of it." The beautiful lady nodded her approval.

Gradually they approached an open plaza which led out to the surrounding territories. Here, at the end of many small booths and shops, a timber building met their gaze; but before they'd caught the slightest sight of it, an ear-splitting roar bellowed in their ears. Feeding time for the wild animals on exhibit seemed to have arrived. The lion unleashed a roar of the jungle and desert, the horses shuddered, and one couldn't avoid noticing how ferociously the king of the wilderness had announced himself in the midst of the cultivated world's peaceful activity. As they approached the booth, they couldn't help seeing the colorful and colossal posters which depicted that strange animal in stark colors and graphic images. This was supposed to evoke an unconquerable desire from the peaceful spectators. A fierce and monstrous tiger sprang at a Moor with the idea of tearing him to shreds. A lion stood there majestically as if he could see no worthy prey; the other wonderfully colored creatures paled next to him.

"When we return, we'll have to dismount and take a closer look at our curious guests," said the Princess.

"It amazes me," replied the Prince, "how man always craves the thrill of terror. The tiger's lying quite peacefully inside his cage, but here he must be portrayed lunging ferociously at a Moor so that the public will believe that they'll see the same spectacle inside; never enough murder and slaughter, blaze and decadence; the street singers have to repeat it on every corner. The good people want to be frightened so that afterwards they can feel how fine and noble it is to catch their breath."

But whatever frightening afterimages the shocking pictures left behind, these vanished the moment they reached the gate and entered the bright countryside. First, the trail led along a river, which at this point was still a narrow body of water carrying only light craft. By degrees, it acquired its name as a great stream, bringing life to distant lands. Then it meandered uphill through well-cultivated orchards and pleasure gardens. Gradually, our travelers looked out upon a visibly well-inhabited region until they were enveloped by bush and woods, refreshing and demarcating their vision with the most pleasing localities. Leading uphill, they were amiably received by a meadow, recently mowed a second time to a velvet appearance and watered by an effervescent and gushing spring from above. From here, they traveled on to a higher, more open view, which they reached by ascending a brisk footpath leading out of the forest. Ahead of them in the distance, they saw the destination of their pilgrimage, the old castle, towering over a group of young trees and crowning the mountain and forest peaks. Through fleeting apertures between the tall trees behind them—for no one reached this point without looking back —they caught to their left a glimpse of the Prince's palace illuminated by the morning sun and the upper, well-built quarter of the town shaded by sparse clouds of smoke; and to their immediate right was the river winding beside pastures and mills to the towns below. A spacious, fertile region stood opposite.

When they'd sated themselves on the panorama, longing only now for a broader, less bounded vista—which tends to happen when we survey the horizon from a high position—they rode across a wide, stony area where the immense ruins faced them like a green-crested summit. At its foot stood a few old trees. Proceeding further, they found themselves directly facing the steepest and most unapproachable slope. Massive crags jutted out of a prehistoric past untouched by any change, solid and firmly fixed, rising into the heights. Fragments that had fallen over time were piled up unevenly in immense slabs and rubble and seemed to prohibit approach even to the most intrepid. The steep and precipitous seems to appeal to youth, however, and young limbs delight in such an undertaking, attack, and conquest. The Princess indicated her desire to attempt it, Honorio stood by her side, and Uncle Friedrich, though more reserved, consented, wishing by no means to show any weakness on his part. The horses were to stay beneath the trees below. They had decided to climb to a specific point where huge, protruding rocks provided a plateau with a bird's eye view which withdrew picturesquely into the converging distance.

The sun, approaching its zenith, imparted the clearest illumination. The palace, with its appurtenances, main building, wings, cupola, and towers was most stately; the upper half of the town appeared in full breadth. The lower part could easily be seen as well; in fact, even the booths in the marketplace could be distinguished through the telescope. Honorio was always accustomed to carrying this useful instrument. They peered up and down the river, which divided the alternating patches of fertile land into terraced mountains on this side and on the other into gently rolling plains and modest hills. Countless villages could be seen, and it had long been the custom to argue about their number and how many could be perceived from up here.

A cheerful lull rested upon the great stretch of land—when Pan sleeps at noon, as the ancients say—and all of nature holds its breath not to wake him.

"It's not the first time," said the Princess, "that I've observed how pure and tranquil nature looks from such a high and all-encompassing station. It gives one the impression that nothing in the world were contrary; then, when one returns to human habitation, be it aristocratic or plebeian, broad or narrow, there's always something to fight, to contend with, to settle, and to rearrange."

Honorio, who had been peering through the telescope at the town, shouted, "Look! look! The market's on fire!" They looked and noticed some smoke, though daylight blanched the flames. "The fire's spreading!" he shouted, still looking through the spyglass. Then the disaster also became noticeable to the Princess's unaided eyes. Here and there they could see a red glow of flames; smoke rose in the sky.

Uncle Friedrich spoke: "Let's go back. This is not good. I've always dreaded reliving that calamity a second time."

When they had descended as far as the horses, the Princess said to the older Prince, "Ride ahead quickly, but not without the groom; leave Honorio with me and we'll follow closely behind you." The Uncle sensed the reason, indeed the necessity, in these words and rode down the barren, stony slope as quickly as the terrain would permit.

When the Princess was seated on her horse, Honorio said, "I beg you to ride slowly, your Highness! The fire fighting provisions in the town, as at the palace, are in the best order. Though such a situation is unexpected and extraordinary, it won't catch them off guard. The terrain is bad here; there are grainy pebbles and short grass. It's dangerous to ride at a gallop, and the fire will be out by the time we've arrived anyway." The Princess did not believe this. She saw the smoke billowing. She believed she'd seen a blaze ignite and had heard a blast. And now her imagination was agitated by all the frightening images that had been so deeply imprinted by noble Friedrich's repeated tale of the market place fire.

That incident had certainly been terrifying, startling, and vivid enough to leave an enduring premonition of recurring misfortune in its wake. That night in the market place, tightly packed with booths, a sudden blaze had consumed one stall after another before those sleeping in and on top of the wobbly huts were shaken from the depths of their dreams. Friedrich, who as a stranger to the town, had arrived quite exhausted and had just fallen asleep, sprang to the window. Everything looked horrifyingly incandescent; flames leaping right and left darted out at him. The houses surrounding the market place, reddened by the reflection, already seemed to be glowing and threatening at any moment to ignite and burst into flames. The forces below raged ceaselessly; boards rattled and slats crackled, canvas sheets went up in smoke and their ragged shreds, scorched and fiery-tipped, batted about up above as though evil spirits were in their element, dancing wantonly, devouring and transmuting themselves over and over, and craving to rise here and there from the embers. And then with a shrieking howl, everyone began to grab whatever was at hand. Servants and priests, along with the gentry, aroused themselves, dragging away flaming bales and wresting from the burning stand whatever else could be thrown into the trunks that, for all their pains, they were forced to abandon as spoils for the rushing flames. How many, wishing the fire's impending roar would cease for only a moment so they could better figure out what to do, were then consumed along with all of their belongings! On one side, everything burned and glowed; on the other, black night stood still. Stubborn characters, people of strong will, fiercely battled the fierce enemy and, with the loss of their hair and eyebrows, they were able to save many things. Unfortunately, this wild confusion now resurrected itself in the beautiful spirit of the Princess. The clear morning horizon now seemed clouded over and her eyes grew gloomy; wood and meadow took on a startling and dreadful appearance.

Riding into the peaceful valley, oblivious to its refreshing briskness, they were but a few steps down from the living source of the brook splashing nearby when the Princess spotted something peculiar way down in the underbrush of the field, something she recognized immediately as the tiger. Bounding up as she'd just recently seen him depicted, he advanced, and compared to the frightful images which had engrossed her, this image made the most bizarre impression. "Flee, Princess, flee!" shouted Honorio. She turned the horse around toward the steep mountain they'd just descended. But the youth, opposite the beast, pulled his pistol and fired when he thought he was close enough. He missed, unfortunately, and the tiger leapt to the side, the horse recoiled, and the enraged animal made its way uphill, directly after the Princess. She galloped up the steep and stony stretch as fast as her horse could climb, unafraid that a gentle creature unused to such exertion would not be able to hold out. Straining under the spurs of its worried rider, it faltered on the small pebbles of the slope and after a last valiant effort fell, powerless, to the ground. The beautiful lady, determined and alert, did not fail to scurry to her feet, and the horse stood upright as well, but the tiger was approaching, though its pace was not very swift. The rough ground and sharp stones seemed to hinder his advance, but Honorio, who was galloping right behind him, seemed to spur and incite him on anew. Both reached the spot at the same time where the Princess stood beside her horse. The horseman bent forward, fired with the second pistol and shot the beast through the head, felling it instantly. Only when it was fully stretched out could its might and fearfulness be truly seen, of which only the corporeal part now remained. Honorio leapt from his horse and knelt down on the animal, extinguishing its last movements and holding his drawn buck-knife in his right hand. The youth was handsome and he'd galloped just as the Princess had often seen him gallop earlier in jousting tournaments; just as his bullet had pierced the Turk's forehead beneath the turban as he rode past the post in riding school; just as he'd speared the Moor's head off the ground with the shining saber as he charged forward. He was adept and successful in all such arts, and these now stood him in good stead.

"Finish him off," said the Princess. "I fear that he'll still hurt you with his claws."

"Forgive me," replied the youth, "he's already dead enough and I don't want to spoil the pelt which shall embellish your sleigh next winter."

"Don't mock!" said the Princess. "Moments such as these reveal the piety dwelling in the depths of a person's heart."

"But I was never so pious as right now; therefore, I think of what would gratify me most: to see this tiger skin serve you as you desire."

"It would always remind me of this awful moment," she replied.

"But isn't it a more innocent token of victory than parading the slain enemy's weapons before the victor?"

"Very well. It will remind me of your boldness and skill. Need I add that you can count on my gratefulness and the Prince's favor for life? But stand up; there's no more life left in the beast. Let's consider the next course of action; by all means, stand up!"

"Since I'm kneeling," replied the youth, "and because I find myself in a position which would be forbidden to me in any other situation, allow me this moment to ask for assurance of the favors and graces that you've granted me. So often I've asked His Majesty, your husband, for a leave of absence and the privilege of extended travel. Whoever is fortunate enough to sit at your table, whomever you honor with permission to take pleasure in your company, that person must have seen the world. Travelers stream here from every region; and whenever a city or an important point of some continent is mentioned, the members of your court are always asked if they themselves have been there. One who hasn't seen it at all is not expected to understand. It's as if the sake of others were the reason to inform oneself."

"Stand up!" the Princess repeated. "I do not gladly wish or request anything contrary to my husband's views, yet if I'm not mistaken, the reasons why you've been detained will soon be retracted. His intention was to see you mature into a self-supporting nobleman, an honor to yourself and the Prince when you're away, as you've honored the court up to the present; and I would think that your deed today is commendable enough a passport as any which a young man could take with him in the world."

Instead of showing any youthful enthusiasm, Honorio's face expressed a certain sadness, but the Princess had neither the time to notice it nor the opportunity to accommodate his sentiments, for a woman holding a boy by the hand came running up the mountain toward our group. No sooner had the brooding Honorio risen to his feet than the woman flung herself upon the dead tiger, wailing and weeping. This behavior, as well as her colorful and peculiar costume, which was nonetheless neat and respectable, revealed at once that she was the mistress and caretaker of the creature stretched out on the ground. The boy, dark-eyed with curly black hair and carrying a flute in his hand, knelt down beside his mother. Though he wept less passionately, he was still deeply moved.

A stream of words, sporadically interrupted like a brook plunging in intervals from rock to rock, followed this unhappy woman's violent outbursts of passion. A natural speech, short and disconnected, expressed itself with power and poignancy. Though it would be a vain attempt to translate it into our dialect, we shall not conceal its general content: "They've murdered you, poor creature! Murdered without cause! You were tame and would have gladly waited for us sitting peacefully, for the pads of your paws caused you pain and your claws had no more strength! You lacked the hot sun to harden them. You were the most beautiful of your kind. Who has ever seen such a regal tiger stretched out so lordly in sleep as you're lying here now dead, to stand up no more. When you would wake up to the morning's early light, open your mouth wide and stretch out your red tongue, you seemed to be smiling at us; and if you roared, you still took your food playfully from a woman's hands, and from the fingers of a child! How long we accompanied you on your journeys, how long your company was essential and valuable to us! Yes, it was! Your voracity brought us each day our daily bread, and our sweet comforts were the gifts of your strength. It will never be the same again. O my soul! O my soul!"

She was still lamenting when horsemen halfway up the mountain near the castle came galloping down the slope. They were soon recognized as the Prince's hunting party, and leading the way was the Prince. They had seen the rising clouds of smoke while hunting in the backwoods on the other side of the mountain, and in the frenzy of heated pursuit had taken the direct route through valleys and ravines toward these gloomy signals. Riding at full speed over the stony clearing, they faltered and stopped short, having now perceived the unexpected group which stood out distinctly on the barren surface. At the moment of recognition, they fell silent, and after they had recovered their bearings, the remaining ambiguities of the sight were elucidated with a few words.

Facing this unique and unprecedented event, the Prince was surrounded by a circle of horsemen and those hastening after on foot. No one hesitated about what action to take and the Prince was busy giving commands and taking charge of the situation when a man dressed like the woman and child in colorful and odd attire made his way into the circle. Now the whole family displayed their grief and bewilderment in unison. The man, however, was restrained; and standing at a respectful distance from the Prince he said, "It's not the time for lamentation. Oh, my Lord and mighty hunter, the lion is also loose, and is making his way toward the mountain here as well; but spare him, have mercy that he not perish like this good creature."

"The lion?" asked the Prince. "You've spotted his tracks?"

"Yes, Sire! A fellow down there who had needlessly taken refuge in a tree directed me up here to the left, but I saw a large troop of people and horses up ahead. Curious and needing help, I hurried here."

"In that case, we must take up the hunt over there," the Prince commanded. "Load your rifles and proceed cautiously. It's no misfortune if you drive it deep into the forest; however, my good man, we really won't be able to indulge this lion of yours. Why were you careless enough to let it escape?"

"The fire broke out," the man replied. "We kept still and sat tight. It spread quickly though it was still far away from us, and we had enough water for our own defense; but then a powder keg blew up and hurled the blaze in our direction and then over us. We reacted too quickly and now we're destitute."

The Prince was still occupied giving directives when everything seemed to be momentarily interrupted. A man was seen hurrying down from the old castle above and was soon recognized as the appointed watchman who, having taken up residence there, guarded the painter's workshop and superintended the laborers. He bounded in out of breath, but soon made himself plain with few words. "The lion's up there behind the upper ringwall, sprawled out in the sunshine at the foot of a century-old beech!" Angrily, however, the man concluded, "Why did I lug my shotgun into town to have it polished yesterday! If I'd had it in my hands, he'd never've stood up again, the hide would've been mine, and I'd've had me somethin' to rightfully brag about all my life."

The Prince had already been in situations before where inescapable harm threatened from several sides, and now his military savvy rescued him here as well. He asked, "Were we to spare your lion, how could you guarantee that it would not endanger my subjects?"

The father replied at once. "My wife and child offer to tame him and keep him quiet until I can bring his cage up here to carry him back safely and unharmed."

The boy seemed ready to play his flute, which being the kind otherwise called a *flute d'amour*, was neatly embouchured like the fife. Whoever understands it can lure from it the most charming notes. In the meantime, the Prince asked the watchman how the lion had climbed up there. "Through the rocky gorge; that's always been the only entrance—an' it should be. We ripped up the two footpaths that used to lead up there, so nobody'd be able to get to the magic castle 'cept through this first narrow path, since Prince Friedrich's of a mind and fancy that it be this way."

Momentarily reflecting as he watched the child, who continued to pipe softly a kind of prelude, the Prince turned to Honorio and said, "You've accomplished much today, now complete the task. Follow the narrow trail, load your rifle and hold it steady, but don't shoot unless you cannot otherwise frighten it back. In the worst case, light a fire if it tries to come down, for that will scare it. The man and woman take responsibility for the rest." Honorio promptly prepared to carry out the orders.

The child continued his melody, though it really could not be called such. It was a sequence of notes without structure which perhaps for this very reason stirred the heart so much. Those surrounding him appeared to be entranced by the tempo of the lyrical style; and then with polite enthusiasm, the father began to speak: "God has given the Prince wisdom and the knowledge that all God's works are wise, each in its own way. Observe the stone cliff, how firmly it stands, motionlessly defying weather and sunshine. Primeval trees adorn its peak, and thus crowned it stares out at the surrounding distance; but if a chunk breaks off, it will not remain what it was. Instead, it shatters into many pieces that cover the slope. But they don't abide there either. They tumble mischievously down to the depths below where the brook gathers them up and conveys them to the river. Neither resisting nor rebelling nor jagged-edged, but smooth and rounded off, they flow swiftly, passing from river to river until they finally reach the ocean where the giants travel in bands and the dwarfs swarm the depths.

"But who praises the Glory of God, whom the stars extol from eternity to eternity! Why do you look out into the surrounding vastness? Observe the bee! Late in the autumn, it still gathers and builds itself a hive, rectangular and horizontal, its own master and journeyman; look at the ant there. It knows its way and is never lost. It builds it up and forms it into an arch, but its efforts are in vain when the horse stamps and paws everything asunder. See! it tramples their balconies and scatters their planks; it snorts impatiently and cannot rest, for the Lord has made the steed the companion of the wind and the confederate of the storm, so that it can carry man wherever he will, and woman wherever she wishes. But the lion emerged in the palm forest, crossing the wilderness with solemn stride. He rules over all the animals there and nothing resists him, though man knows how to tame him, and this most ferocious of beasts stands in awe before the likeness of God, after whom the Lord's attendant angels and servants were also fashioned. For Daniel did not cower in the lion's den; he stood firm and was courageous, and the wild roaring did not interrupt his pious hymn."

The child accompanied this expression of natural enthusiasm with agreeable notes here and there, but when the father had said his piece, the boy began to intone with sonorous throat, bright voice, and a sure-footed rhythm. At this, the father took up the flute and joined in harmony as the boy sang:

> Out of caves, here at the moat,
> the prophet's song I hear.
> To delight him, angels float;
> why should the godly fear?
> Now and then, lion and lioness
> yield unto the angel's hymn;
> ah, the gentle song so righteous
> captivated them.

The father followed the stanza in accompaniment on the flute, and the mother joined in here and there as second voice.

But it was especially impressive when the child then rearranged the lines of the stanza, which heightened their emotional effect without producing a new meaning.

> Angels below and angels above
> delight us with their notes;
> what music of the spheres!
> In the caves and by the moats
> would the child have any fears?
> These gentle songs of righteous love
> won't let misfortune bleat;
> at times, the angels soar above
> and then the task's complete.

Then all three began to sing with power and exaltation:

> His timelessness on earth holds sway,
> over oceans reigns His glance.
> Billows shall ebb and flow away
> and lions become as lambs;
> shining sword, stand still midair;
> faith and hopefulness are sealed;

wonder-working is the prayer,
the prayer when love's revealed.

Everything was still, all things heard, listened, and only when the tones receded could their impression perhaps be noted and studied. Everyone seemed tempered, each heart touched in its own way. The Prince, as if only now able to overlook the trouble which had threatened him earlier, looked down at his wife who, leaning at his side, withdrew the embroidered handkerchief to cover her eyes. She felt better now that her youthful breast had been relieved of the pressure with which the preceeding minutes had burdened her. A perfect silence ruled the crowd, and the dangers of the fire below and the emergence of a questionably composed lion above seemed to have been forgotten.

Giving them a nod to lead the horses in closer, the Prince first brought some motion back to the group; then he turned to the mother and said, "So you believe that your song and the child's accompaniment on the flute will pacify the stray lion when you find him, and that you'll be able to bring him back safely and unharmed under lock and key?"

She solemnly affirmed this and the watchman was sent along with them as a guide. The prince then hurried off with some of the party and the Princess followed more slowly with the rest; the mother and son, however, climbed the steep slope ahead of the accompanying watchman who had armed himself with a rifle.

In front of the entrance to the gorge, which opened out into the passage to the castle, they found the hunters busy gathering dry twigs in case they needed to kindle a large fire. "It's not necessary," said the woman. "Everything will turn out to the good without all that."

Further ahead, they spotted Honorio sitting atop the wall, his double-barrel weapon resting across his lap, posted as though ready for anything that might happen. Yet he barely seemed to notice them approaching and sat there as though lost in deep thought, looking around distractedly. The woman spoke to him requesting that he not let the fire be kindled, but he seemed to pay little attention to her words. She continued to speak in a more spirited way and exclaimed, "Handsome young man, you've killed my tiger. I don't curse you, but if you save my lion, fine young man, I'll bless you."

Honorio stared straight ahead at the point where the sun began to sink in its path. "You look toward the west," shouted the woman, "and are wise to do so, for there's much to do; but hurry, don't hesitate, you will overcome your obstacles, but first overcome yourself." He seemed to smile at this. The woman climbed further, but she couldn't help looking back at the young man. Reddish sunlight glowed across his face. She believed that she'd never seen such a handsome youth.

"If that boy of yours," said the watchman, "can lure and pacify the lion by singing and playin' a flute, as you seem to think, then it'll be real easy for us to subdue him, 'cause that big brute's lain down near the broken vault where we've cleared a path to the castle yard, seein' how the main gate's fallen to rubble. If the boy can lure 'im in there, I can seal off the opening without any trouble, and then he can slip away from the beast up the little winding staircase which he'll see over in the corner. We'll hide ourselves, but I'll take up a position so that my bullet can come to his rescue at any moment."

"All these considerations are unnecessary," she replied. "God and ingenuity, piety and good fortune must do their best."

"Could be," the watchman responded, "but I know my duties. First I'll lead you down through a difficult trail up to the wall, directly across from the entrance which I've already mentioned. The boy can climb down into what's like a theater arena and lure the pacified brute into it." And this is just what happened. The watchman and mother hiding up above saw how the boy walked down the staircase into the open courtyard and then disappeared into the dark opening facing it. His flute playing, which could be heard at once, receded little by little and finally ceased. The pause was ominous and the old hunter, familiar with danger, felt uneasy about the unusual human affair. He said that he personally would have preferred to face the dangerous beast himself; nonetheless, the mother, looking serene as she leaned forward and listened, displayed no trace of disquiet.

Finally, they heard the flute again, and the boy emerged from the hollow with sparkling, contented eyes. The lion followed behind him, though slowly and, so it seemed, with some difficulty. Here and there, it indicated its desire to lie down, but the boy paraded it in a semi-circle through the few sparsely-leaved trees of brilliant hue until finally,

as if illuminated in the last rays of sunlight which streamed in through
a chink in the ruins, he sat down and began his tranquil song, whose
repetition we cannot deny ourselves.

Out of caves, here at the moat,
the prophet's song I hear.
To delight him, angels float,
why should the godly fear?
Now and then, lion and lioness
yield unto the angels' hymn;
ah, the gentle song so righteous
captivated them.

Meanwhile, the lion lay down by the child's side and put its
heavy right forepaw in the boy's lap. The boy petted it gently as he
continued to sing, but he soon noticed that a sharp thorn was stuck
between the pads. Carefully, he withdrew the offending spine and
with a smile unwrapped the silken scarf from his neck and bandaged
the animal's paw. His mother leaned back with outstretched arms
and, perhaps out of habit, might have clapped and cheered, had the
watchman's coarse grasp not reminded her that the danger was not
over yet.

After piping a few notes in prelude, the child sang on gloriously:

His timelessness on earth holds sway,
over oceans reigns his glance.
Billows shall ebb and flow away
and lions become as lambs;
shining sword, stand still midair;
faith and hopefulness are sealed;
wonder-working is the prayer,
the prayer when love's revealed.

If it's possible to imagine an expression of friendliness and grate-
ful satisfaction in the features of such a fierce creature, the tyrant of
the forest, the despot of the animal kingdom, then such an expression
could now be discerned. In his transformation, the child really looked
like a mighty and triumphant conqueror; but the lion did not look
vanquished, for his strength remained concealed within himself, like
one who has submitted to his own peaceful will. The child piped on,
adding and interlacing new verses as he sang:

## Novelle

So guide good children safe and sound,
Blessed Angel, joyfully,
and every wicked will confound;
further Beauty's every deed;
and ban the tyrant from the bower,
and from the son upon your knee;
charm this forest tyrant's power
with holiness and melody.

# ⦿ The Magic Flute ⦿
## A comic opera fragment

*Day. A forest. A rocky grotto where a portal has been hewn.
From the forest.*

*Enter: Monostatos and Moors.*

MONOSTATOS

O comrades, sing praises,
rejoice in our gain!
We've come to our Goddess
in triumph again.

CHORUS

Success has been with us,
good luck helped us win!
We've come to our Goddess
in triumph again.

MONOSTATOS

We did it sly-handed,
we wormed ourselves in;
of what she's commanded,
the first part is done.

CHORUS

We did it sly-handed,
we wormed ourselves in;
and what she's commanded
soon will be done.

MONOSTATOS

O Goddess! sealed from every eye
in the vaults, who dwells all alone,
soon in the loftiest air of sky,

defying the light upon your throne,
O hear out your friend! in the future, your groom!
What hinders you, omnipresent might,
what holds you back, O Queen of the Night!
from instantly spreading your shadows of gloom?

*Thunderclap. Monostatos and Moors fall to the ground. Darkness. Clouds emerge from the portal and envelop it.*

THE QUEEN
Who calls me out?
Who tempts me with speech?
Who hazards this stillness with voices to breach?
I hear nothing—Ha! alone I must be!
The world should indeed be silent 'bout me!

*The clouds overshadow the theater and envelop Monostatos and the Moors, who can still be seen.*

Cloud up, you billows,
and cover the earth,
that gloominess gain
a more sinister girth!
Terror and hailing,
Sorrow and wailing
faintly recede; let fright
close the hymn to the night
with silence and death.

MONOSTATOS AND CHORUS
Before your throne here,
stationed to serve, are—

QUEEN
Do you, disciples, appear
before me once more?

MONSTATOS
Yes, your disciple,
my love, it's he.

QUEEN

Am I found out?

CHORUS

Goddess, it's thee!

QUEEN

Spiral, you firebolts,
rage ceaselessly, thunder,
shatter the smothering
nighttime asunder.
Comets, stream onward
and down through the skies!
Wandering stars,
ken the stars in your eyes.
Light up the loftily
satisfied rage.

MONSTATOS AND CHORUS

Look! comets,
they fall through the skies.
Wandering stars
ken the stars in their eyes,
and from the poles
arises the blaze.

*The Queen stands in all her glory as a light from the north shines from
center stage. Comets, St. Elmo's Fire, and balls of light crisscross in the
clouds. The form, color, and secret symmetry of all this must have a
frightening but agreeable effect.*

MONOSTATOS

Before the world in festive light,
splendidly you'll soon appear.
In the solar realm, you wield your might.
Pamina and Tamino still shed their tears;
their highest bliss interred in the night.

QUEEN

Their newborn son, is he in my hands?

MONOSTATOS

Not yet, but soon we'll meet your demands;
I read the signs in the stars' savage fight.

QUEEN

Not yet in my hands? What did you, then?

MONOSTATOS

O Goddess, have mercy upon your men!
We bade farewell to the king in lament.
Now you can loathe her to your heart's content.
Hark! Climbing his throne, here comes the morn
and hope approaches, sweet,
who promised connubial trust a treat,
the long-entreated first son born.
The maidens were with full festoons,
the flower'd wreathes did swell;
in pageant sacrifice, and damsels danced, in revel.
Their new costumes pleased them all the more.
While the women were roused with eagerness keen
as matrons to bear in mind the queen,
invisibly, we wormed across the palace floor.
We heard, "A son, a son!" and opened, as they screamed,
the gold sarcophagus that was our care.
The darkness poured out, shrouding everyone there;
each one tripped and shook and dreamed.
The mother had yet her boy to behold,
the father had yet his son to admire,
but I grabbed him quickly, with a hand of fire
and shut him at once in that casket of gold.
And ever darker grows the night
when we see with the tiger's eye.
But oh, I don't know what cruel might
resists us with its power.
The gold casket burdens us more—

CHORUS
Grows heavier in our hands.

MONOSTATOS
Grows heavier than ever before.
We can't finish the work she demands.

CHORUS
It pulls us down to the floor.

MONOSTATOS
It's firmly fixed there, we can't lift it away.
Sarastro's magic is blocking its way.

CHORUS
We fear the spell ourselves and so must flee.

QUEEN
You cowards, is that how you act?
My rage—

CHORUS
Your rage, O Queen, you must withhold!

MONOSTATOS
With sapience and skill so bold,
I press your seal to the grave of gold
and shut the lad forever in your care,
which no one can undo.
Then you'll have him in your snare
and the stiff little dear will belong to you.
His form lies there, dead, and frightens the day.
With anthems forbidding, we saunter away.

CHORUS
Should the mother ever see,
should she ever see the son,
then tear his fate away,
tear his fate away at once.

Should the father ever see,
should he ever see the son,
then tear his fate away,
tear his fate away at once.

MONOSTATOS

In the distance, then, I did discern
the casket, light as feathers.
They're bringing him to a fraternal order
where he'll shut himself in to teach wisdom and learn.
With newfound craft and strength, your servant perseveres.
Even in the holy spheres,
your hate and curses hold their sway.
If the consorts see themselves, let madness entrance,
and the sight of their child be a sight that enchants,
and forever tears that child away.

QUEEN, MONOSTATOS, AND CHORUS

If the parents ever see,
if they catch themselves in sight,
grab their souls at once,
O madness and fright.

If the parents ever see,
if they ever see the son,
tear their fate away,
tear their fate away at once.

*Women enter carrying a golden frame which supports the golden sar-*
*cophagus. An exquisite carpet is suspended from the frame. Other*
*women carry an ornate canopy over the sarcophagus.*

CHORUS OF WOMEN

We wander on in quiet fear,
and grieve at every lust;
a child is there, a son is here,
and worries crowd the breast.

A LADY

So wander forth, do not stand still.

This is what the wise men will.
Have faith in them and blindly obey;
the child shall live as long as you stray.

CHORUS

O woeful, captivated boy,
what shall become of you.
Your mother's not allowed her joy,
your father's been denied it, too.

A LADY

And the consorts split painfully asunder.
And may take no comfort, heart in heart.
He wanders off; she cries there, left apart;
Sarastro still lulls the house to slumber.

CHORUS

O slumber gently, slumber sweet,
you long awaited son!
Leave this crypt, and with a leap
ascend your father's throne.

A LADY

It's time to roam, here comes the King
You can hear wailing in the empty room ring;
by now he's sensed the gloom round his throne,
yet does not see the crypt of his precious son.

*They cross the stage*

TAMINO

When the boy is softly smiling
at the father from his bassinet,
and the morning breeze is wiling
all around his charming silhouette,
yes! for this gift, he gives thanks to fate.
This good means more than all his estate.
And he lives, and loved shall be
the one that gives love back to me.

WOMEN (*in the distance*)
O he lives and loved shall be
the one that gives love back to thee.

TAMINO
Dawn is breaking, day is nigh
in Aurora's purple light.
Oh! Dreadful thunder claps the sky
and veils the scene of joy with night.
And what these fates of mine revealed,
a golden grave too soon concealed.

WOMEN (*in the distance*)
Oh, what these fates of ours revealed,
a golden grave too soon concealed.

TAMINO
I hear the bearers of my sweet draw nigh.
Come closer! Let's unite and sigh.
O say! How does Pamina bear the news?

A LADY
She's lost without the gods' fine joys.
She sighs for you and grieves for the boy.

TAMINO
O tell me, does my prisoned bliss still breathe?
Does he move yet in his magic place?
Give me hope to see my treasure's face!
Oh give my baby back to me!

LADIES
We listen as we wander
with feelings woebegotten.
His restless moves we ponder—
too strange to be forgotten.
We feel inside what's yearning,
we see the casket churning.
We hearken but can say no more

of goodly omens seen before.
At night when every sound has died,
we hear the babbling child inside.

TAMINO

Guard him, you gods, with miraculous care!
Revive him with drink, feed him your fare!
And demonstrate your trust to me,
always bestir yourselves to act.
Sarastro's word will set us free
and consecrate its holy pact.

Listen to the smallest murmur
and inform the worried father
of the slightest little gest.

TAMINO AND CHORUS

And delivered from hazard's way,
at the mother's breast he'll pray.
Soon an angel, there he'll rest.

*Woods and rocks. A hut in the background. A golden waterfall on one side, a flock of birds on the other.*

PAPAGENO *and* PAPAGENA *sit on opposite sides of the stage with backs turned toward one another.*

SHE (*stands up and goes to him*)
What is it then, my dearest little man?

HE (*sitting*)
I'm vexed and nasty, let me be!

SHE
Aren't I your dearest little hen?
Don't you want to be with me?

HE
I'm vexed and nasty, vexed and nasty!

SHE

He's vexed and nasty, vexed and nasty!

BOTH

The whole wide world just isn't fair.

SHE (*sits off to the side*)

HE (*stands up and goes to her*)
What is it then, dear wife, my love?

SHE

I'm vexed and nasty, don't come near!

HE

Aren't you still my sweet dear dove?
Will our love just disappear?

SHE

I'm vexed and nasty, vexed and nasty!

HE (*distancing himself*)
I'm vexed and nasty, vexed and nasty!

BOTH

What happened to our love so dear?

| | |
|---|---|
| HE | My child! my child! let's come to our senses just a bit. Aren't we being really ungrateful toward our benefactors by carrying on this way? |
| SHE | Indeed! I agree, and yet it can't be helped. |
| HE | Why then aren't we satisfied? |
| SHE | Because we aren't gay. |
| HE | Didn't the Prince give us that precious flute as a wedding present for luring the tastiest animals to our dinner table? |
| SHE | And didn't you present me with that splendid glockenspiel on the second day of our honeymoon. I only need to tap |

it, and all the birds fall into the trap at once. The doves sail perfectly barbequed into our mouths.

HE    The jack rabbits jump onto the table fully smoked and garnished. And Sarastro conjured up that bountiful fountain of wine by our cottage—and yet, we're still not satisfied.

SHE   (*sighing*) Yes! and it's no wonder.

HE    (*sighing*) Quite so, no wonder.

SHE   We're lacking—

HE    Unfortunately, we're lacking—

SHE   (*crying*) We're really so unhappy!

HE    (*crying*) Quite so, so unhappy!

SHE   (*with increased blubbering*) The pretty,

HE    (*with increased blubbering*) pleasing,

SHE   charming,

HE    little,

SHE   Pa-

HE    Pa-

SHE   Papa-

HE    Papa-

SHE   Oh, the pain will do me in.

HE    I may not live much longer.

SHE   I thought they'd be here by now.

HE    They're already hopping around.

SHE   How pleasing it would be.

HE    First a little Papageno.

SHE   And then a little Papagena.

HE       Papageno.

SHE      Papagena.

HE       Now where do you think they could be?

SHE      They simply haven't shown up.

HE       That's truly a misfortune! Had I only hanged myself when
         the time was ripe.

SHE      If I'd only stayed an old lady!

BOTH     Oh, we poor unfortunates!

CHORUS (*behind the scene*)
You good little creatures,
why do you dismay?
You comical birdies,
be happy and gay!

HE
Aha!

SHE
Aha!

BOTH
The boulders are ringing,
they sing one and all.
They're ringing
they're singing
with forest and hall.

CHORUS
Take care of your business,
in silence, enjoy,
the gods are bestowing—
(*pause*)

HE
The Pa?

CHORUS (*as echo*)
The Pa, Pa, Pa.

HE
The Papagenos?

SHE
The Papagenas?
(*pause*)

CHORUS
The gods are presenting
you parents a boy.

HE
Come, let's pull ourselves in line
that this melancholia disappear.
But first, let's drink a glass of wine—

*They go to the fountain and drink.*

BOTH
Now, let's pull ourselves in line.
Melancholia, disappear!

*He takes the flute and looks around as if he were looking for game.
She sits in the little portico by the flock of birds and picks up the
glockenspiel.*

HE (*playing*)

SHE (*singing*)
O Great spirit of the Light!
Bring our hunt good luck!

SHE (*plays*) BOTH (*singing*)
Let the troop of colored birds
descend upon the flock.

HE (*plays*) SHE (*sings*)
See! the lions roaming there,
roaming keeps them fresh.

SHE (*plays*) HE (*sings*)
But far too brawny for my taste.
What a gristly flesh!

HE (*plays*) SHE (*sings*)
Hear the little birdies flap,
flapping in the nest.

SHE (*plays*) HE (*sings*)
Keep playing! these little birdies
taste the very best.
Hens are hopping in the fields,
chickens fat and pretty.

HE (*plays*) SHE (*plays and sings*)
Bunnies jump! Here come the hares!
Don't stop your little ditty.

*Hares and rabbits appear on the rocks. Lions, bears, and apes also approach, and stand in front of the parrots.*

SHE (*plays*) HE (*sings*)
Were I only rid of bears!
and apes, accursed and randy!
Bears are just so thick and dumb,
and apes such skinny dandies.

*Parrots can be seen in the trees.*

SHE (*plays and sings*)
And the parrot troops fly by,
traveling in migration.
Brilliant colors fan the sky;
to eat, though, no temptation.

HE (*has, in the meantime, trapped the hares and is carrying one on a large ladle*)
See, I've snatched myself a hare,
lured it from the rabble.

SHE (*has just shut the snare where the fluttering feathers of birds can be seen*)
See, the fattened birdies here
are tangled in their gaggle.
*She takes out a bird and brings it to him, holding it by the wings.*

BOTH
True, my child, we try to live
our life from day to day.
As we wander to our hut,
let's be cheerful, let's be gay.

CHORUS (*hidden*)
You comical birdies
be happy and gay.
Redouble your paces,
your prayers will be blessed;
the bungalow's graces
shall grant you the best.

*HE and SHE join in the repetition of this stanza.*
Redouble our paces,
our prayers will be blessed.
Our bungalow's graces
shall grant us the best.

TEMPLE
Assembly of the Priests.

CHORUS
A man can always look and choose!
But does choice bring any gain?
The clever falter, wise men lose

and double all their pain.
Acting proper,
upright posture,
are the noble-minded choice.
Should no selection
cause dejection,
chance will also raise its voice.

*Sarastro enters before the end of the song and joins them. When the song fades out, the Speaker enters and walks over to Sarastro.*

SPEAKER   Our brother stands before the northern gate of our holy shrine. He has completed the year of pilgrimage and wishes to be admitted. He has transferred the special signs which demonstrate his worthiness for re-admission to our circle.

*He presents Sarastro with a round crystal tied by a ribbon.*

SARASTRO   This mysterious stone is still bright and clear. Had our brother failed in his mission, it would have appeared murky. Lead the returning brother onward!
*Exit: Speaker*
Behind these quiet walls, a man learns to look into himself and explore the deep recesses of his soul. He prepares himself to perceive the voice of the gods. But only the wanderer who has roamed over the wide fields of the earth can learn to recognize the sublime language of nature and the sounds of humankind in need. For this reason, we abide by our rule of sending a pilgrim out into the raw world each year. The lottery decides and the righteous obey. After I've entrusted my diadem to the worthy Tamino, who will rule in my place with youthful vigor and precocious wisdom, I too, for the first time, will be in the same position as each of you who must reach into the holy vessel and submit to the fate of the pronouncement.
*Enter: Speaker and Pilgrim*

PILGRIM    Hail to thee, Father! Hail to you, brothers!

ALL    Hail to you!

SARASTRO    The crystal shows me that you return pure of heart and without blame. Now tell your brothers what you've learned. Add to their wisdom. But first, wait for the appropriate moment when you've entrusted your robe and crystal to the one whom the will of the gods selects for the pilgrimage from our happy society.

*He gives the crystal back to the Pilgrim. Two priests carry a portable altar, which supports a flat, golden vessel. The altar must be high enough so that no one can see into the vessel.*

## CHORUS

SARASTRO    (*unrolling the lottery scroll*) The lottery has fallen to me, and I shall not hesitate a single moment to submit to its command. Indeed, my premonitions have been borne out. The gods want to distance me from your midst in order to test us. The moment the powers of the malevolent forces have become operative, I'll be called away. The shell of the Good will become light in my absence. But hold fast, persevere, don't waver from the steady course, and we'll soon see each other again.

> I gave the crown to my minion,
> I gave it to the worthy man.
> But still I keep dominion
> to serve you all the best I can.
> Yet, even that's now torn away;
> I have to leave you all today.
> From this holy shrine, I must depart;
> all my sons, take heart.
> You sons, I bid farewell.
> Guard Wisdom's exalted dell.
> From this sacred Hall and ground,
> I leave, a pilgrim onward bound.

*During this aria, Sarastro hands over his robe and high priest's emblems, which are carried off with the golden vessel. In return, he receives the pilgrim's garb, the ribbon attached to the crystal is placed around his neck, and he takes the staff in his hand. During the various parts of the aria, the composer will know how to space the caesuras.*

CHORUS
Now who rules
the sacred hall and ground?
He leaves, a pilgrim onward bound.

*The priests remain standing on both sides of the middle altar.*

SARASTRO
Life was just a day to me,
my brothers, there with you.
So praise the joy around thee,
submit yourselves supinely,
then raise yourselves sublimely,
for God may bid that, too.
We must be cleaving,
our exit's imposed.
O how I am grieving!
I must stay composed!
O what a blow!
(*exit*)

CHORUS
You hallowed hallways,
hear out our sad refrain;
the brighter days
no longer do acclaim
Sarastro's word:
no instruction's heard
in solemn locations
'midst high obligations.
And verity's
no longer on earth.

Its clarity
cannot disperse.
Your higher path
is now in sight,
but we're engulfed
by deepest night.

## A FESTIVE PROCESSION

*Pamina with her entourage. The casket is carried along with them.
In pursuance of an oracle, she dedicates it to the sun. The casket is
placed on the altar. Prayer, earthquake. The altar along with the cas-
ket sink into the earth. Pamina's despair. The scene is arranged in
such a way that the actress can express a meaningful spectrum of
emotions with help from the music.*

### FOREST AND ROCKS. PAPAGENO'S DWELLING.

*They've discovered big beautiful eggs in the hut. They suspect that
special birds might be hidden inside. The poet should be cautious that
the amusement in this scene remain within the limits of propriety.
Sarastro approaches them. Following a few mystical utterances about
natural forces, a lowly rock emerges from the earth. A fire burns in
its center. Following Sarastro's command, a comfortable nest is pre-
pared on the rock, the eggs are placed on it and covered with flow-
ers. Sarastro steps back. The eggs begin to swell. They crack open
and children tumble out one after another: two boys and a girl. Their
first gestures amongst themselves and vis-à-vis their elders should pro-
vide an opportunity for poetic and musical jests. Sarastro goes over
to them. A few words on education. Then he describes Pamina and
Tamino's sad predicament. After the casket has sunk, Pamina searches
out her consort. When they catch sight of each other, they fall into
a sleep from which they can waken only for the short time required
to abandon themselves to despair. Sarastro calls the cheerful family
back to the court to lighten its distress with jokes. Papageno in par-
ticular is to bring the flute in order to test its healing power. Sarastro,
who alone remains behind, scales the mountain during an aria.*

### ANTECHAMBER IN THE PALACE

*Two ladies and two gentlemen are walking back and forth.*

119

TUTTI

Quiet, that no one cause a commotion.
Let the singing drift by, dreamy in motion!
You're troubled, in guarded anxiety,
should the King fall ill, then so too will we.

THIRD LADY (*coming quickly*)

Would you like to hear the news today,
can I tell you the latest tale?
Soon we won't have to weep and wail.
The mother's been appeased, they say.

THIRD GENTLEMAN (*coming quickly to join them*)

And Papageno, so they say,
has found the greatest treasure:
great nuggets of gold and silver
as big as ostrich eggs.

FIRST TUTTI

Quiet, whatever possessed you to bring
news while we sing out the pains of the King?
(*pause*)
But go ahead, speak, make yourself known.

THIRD LADY

Do you want to hear the latest news?—

THIRD GENTLEMAN

And Papageno, so they say—

THIRD LADY

Let me tell you the latest—

THIRD GENTLEMAN

has found the greatest treasure—

FOURTH LADY (*coming quickly to join them*)

Though Sarastro can be found,
he's disappeared, I've heard.

He's only gone to gather herbs,
to heal and make us sound.

FOURTH GENTLEMAN (*coming quickly to join them*)
The happy hours I sound,
when all our pains are past;
for the Prince has now been found,
and they bring him here at last.

TUTTI (*repeating her story*)
Quiet, why do you want to bring us these rumors?
Help us sing out the pains of the rulers.
If only they were true and sound.

*The last four join in, repeating their news to smaller groups.*

*PAPAGENO and PAPAGENA (who are arguing with a guard)*

PAPAGENO       No one shall hold me back.

PAPAGENA       Nor I.

PAPAGENO       I'd rather have rendered service to the King than
               have your whiskers start growing. They make you
               look so grim.

PAPAGENA       And I did many favors for the Queen when the
               evil Moor still had her in his clutches. Certainly,
               she'd no longer recognize me, for I was old and
               ugly then. Now, I'm young and pretty.

PAPAGENO       Since I'm inside for once, I don't want to go out
               again.

PAPAGENA       And since I'm here, I'll stay.

GENTLEMAN      See the plumed pair there! As if they'd been sum-
               moned. (*to the guard*) Let them alone! The King
               and Queen will welcome them.

PAPAGENO       A thousand thanks, my Lord! We've heard that the
               situation here has taken a turn for the worse.

GENTLEMAN    And we've heard that all goes quite well with you.

PAPAGENO    Till things are better, I'll live.

LADY    Is it true that you've found the splendid eggs?

PAPAGENO    Certainly.

GENTLEMAN    Golden ostrich eggs?

PAPAGENO    None other.

LADY    Are you familiar with the bird that laid them?

PAPAGENO    Not yet.

LADY    They must be splendid eggs.

PAPAGENO    Priceless.

GENTLEMAN    How many have you found so far?

PAPAGENO    About two to three and a half score.

LADY    And all solid?

PAPAGENO    Except for the ones which are translucently bright.

GENTLEMAN    My dearest Papageno, do you have a portion for me?

PAPAGENO    I'd be happy to give you some.

LADY    I'd love to have a pair for my natural science cabinet.

PAPAGENO    They're at your service.

LADY    In that case, I have a dozen friends, all naturalists, who have an especially excellent understanding of noble metals.

PAPAGENO    All of them shall be satisfied.

GENTLEMAN    You're an excellent chap.

PAPAGENO    It's nothing. The eggs are the least of my concerns.

|          |                                                                                  |
|----------|----------------------------------------------------------------------------------|
|          | I'm just as much a merchant now that I'm larger as I was when I was smaller.      |
| LADY     | Where is your merchandise?                                                        |
| PAPAGENO | Outside, beyond the castle yard. I had to leave it there.                         |
| LADY     | Of course, because of the toll.                                                   |
| PAPAGENO | They had no idea how much to claim.                                               |
| GENTLEMAN | They're certainly quite valuable.                                               |
| PAPAGENO | Priceless.                                                                        |
| LADY     | They could be assessed by the egg.                                               |
| PAPAGENO | Of course; the eggs are the source of value.                                    |
| GENTLEMAN | (*to the lady*) We must have him as a friend, we must help them through.        |

*PAPAGENO and PAPAGENA exit. The others fade back. They carry golden bird cages with winged children inside.*

PAPAGENO and PAPAGENA
Of all the pretty wares
that are traveling to the fairs,
none could please you more
than the ones we have in store
for you from lands across the sea.
Listen, while we sing to thee,
and watch the pretty birds!
These birdies are for sale.

PAPAGENA (*letting one out*)
Take a look at this big bird.
He's comical and so absurd.
He lightly hops so cheerfully
from the bushes, from the tree.
Soon he'll perch upon that limb

so now we shall not flatter him.
O see the cheerful birdy,
The birdy is for sale.

PAPAGENO (*displaying another*)
Now watch out for this little tweet;
he wants to look like he's discreet,
though he's silly and absurd;
no better than the bigger bird.
But, when all is hushed and still,
he shows the very best of will.
This silly little birdy,
this birdy is for sale.

PAPAGENA (*displaying the third*)
O see the little dovey,
the dearest turtle lovely!
The females act so gracefully,
so sensibly and mannerly.
They love to preen and spruce.
They love to put your love to use.
The gentle little birdies
are sitting here for sale.

BOTH OF THEM
We wish to sing no praises.
Our birds stand up to all your mazes.
They're in love with all things new,
but to see if they are true,
don't try your seals and letters.
All these birdies have their feathers.
How pleasing are these birdies!
How thrilling every sale!

*The last lines of each verse are repeated in part by the children, the elders, and the chorus at the composer's discretion.*

LADY          They're certainly attractive enough, but is that all there is?

PAPAGENA    That's everything, and I would've thought it sufficient.

GENTLEMAN    Don't you have some of the eggs in the basket? I'd prefer them more than the birds.

PAPAGENO    I believe so. However, should one be allowed to speak the truth in this truth-loving society, then one would have to confess that a few boasts have been made.

GENTLEMAN    Please speak freely.

PAPAGENO    I must confess that this is all the wealth we have.

LADY    That'll certainly go far.

GENTLEMAN    And the eggs?

PAPAGENO    Only the shells remain, for all these have just crawled out of them.

GENTLEMAN    And what about the remaining two and a half score?

PAPAGENO    That was only a figure of speech.

LADY    Then very few would remain for yourselves.

PAPAGENO    A pretty little wife, happy children and a good sense of humor, who has more?

GENTLEMAN    So when it comes right down to it, you're still nothing more than a buffoon.

PAPAGENO    And for that reason, indispensable.

GENTLEMAN    Perhaps this amusement could entertain the King and Queen?

LADY    Not in the least. It would probably only remind them of unhappy memories.

PAPAGENO    And yet Sarastro sent me here for that very reason.

125

GENTLEMAN   Sarastro? Where did you see Sarastro?

PAPAGENO   In our mountains.

GENTLEMAN   Was he searching for herbs?

PAPAGENO   Not that I know of.

GENTLEMAN   But did you see him bending over at times?

PAPAGENO   Yes, especially when he was stumbling.

GENTLEMAN   Such a holy man does not stumble. He bends over for a reason.

PAPAGENO   I'm satisfied with that.

GENTLEMAN   He's looking for herbs, perhaps stones, and he's coming here to cure the King and Queen.

PAPAGENO   But not today, at least, for he expressly ordered me to go to the palace, to take the renowned magic flute, and to strike up a tune for your Majesties when they awaken. In this way, I can at least ward off their pain for a little while.

LADY   One has to try everything.

GENTLEMAN   The hour of Awakening approaches. Try your best. Your efforts will not go unthanked or unrewarded.

PAMINA and TAMINO

Under a canopy, sleeping in two easy chairs. In order not to disturb the pathetic impression, Papagena and the children exit. Papageno stays partly hidden in the wings where he plays the flute and emerges periodically into view.

PAMINA (*waking to the sound of the flute*)
By my side, my loving sleeper
sweetly sleeping, softly waking
soon will see the charming sight.

TAMINO (*waking*)

126

O, that could make the weeper
glad and keep his heart from breaking,
but what plagues my delight?

CHORUS
Play, Papageno, play!
for his pain returns, despite.

PAMINA (*arising and descending the stairs*)
Animated by my lover
rousing me to action
from the gentle shade of slumber
to this life of rash reaction,
and to duty, O what delight!

TAMINO (*arising and descending the stairs*)
Let our glancing lover's eyes
spur us on to deeds of honor,
and calmly well-advised
consecrate with lively valor.
O my rising chest feels light!

*They embrace. Pause, especially the flute.*

CHORUS
Papageno, Papageno,
play your flute without cessation!
Keep it up, you must hold out!

PAPAGENO
But let me get some inspiration!
My breath is almost all played out.

TAMINO and PAMINA (*distancing themselves from one another*)
Do you know what they have taken!
O how empty is our house!

CHORUS
Play, Papageno, play,

Keep it up, you must hold out!
*Papageno plays.*

TAMINO and PAMINA (*amiably approaching again*)
Nothing really has been taken.
Grand and wealthy is our house.

PAPAGENO
Now my breath is all played out!

CHORUS
Keep it up, you must hold out!

PAMINO and TAMINO
O how empty is our house!

*It is entirely up to the composer's discretion to alternate and repeat the transitions from satisfaction and joy to pain and despair occasioned by the foregoing verses.*

*Priests are coming. It's up to the composer to decide whether to introduce only two or the entire chorus. I propose the latter. They give information about the child's whereabouts.*

PRIEST
In the deepest earthly chasms
here's the water, here, the flames,
then the watchman without pity,
then the monster no one tames,
'twixt the living, 'twixt the dead,
half unsouled
with thirsts untold
dwells the boy.
Hear his prayers!
Woe! in thirst he pines away.
Save your son without delay!

EVERYONE
What a dreadful calm is forming
all around us suddenly!

What a muffled, distant swarming!
What an agitated storming!
like the storm upon the sea.
Ever louder from afar,
all the elements grow bold.
What a night inveils the gold
and airy heaven;
and then each star
vanishes from vision.

*Subterranean cavern. The altar and the sarcophagus are in the center*
*as they were when they sank. Armed guards lean against two pillars*
*and seem to be sleeping. Chains running from the pillars are attached*
*to the lions resting at the foot of the altar. All is dark; the translucent*
*sarcophagus illuminates the scene.*

CHORUS (*hidden from view*)
We sentence and we penalize:
the watchman shall not close his eyes;
the heavens glow so red.
The lions can't be resting,
if the crypt stands any testing,
the boy shall then be dead.

*The lions rise and pace back and forth on their chains.*

FIRST WATCHMAN (*without moving*)
Brother, are you awake?

SECOND WATCHMAN (*without moving*)
I hear you.

FIRST WATCHMAN
Are we alone?

SECOND WATCHMAN
Who knows?

FIRST WATCHMAN
Is it daylight?

129

SECOND WATCHMAN
Perhaps, yes.

FIRST WATCHMAN
Is night falling?

SECOND WATCHMAN
There it is.

FIRST WATCHMAN
The time passes.

SECOND WATCHMAN
But how?

FIRST WATCHMAN
No doubt, the hour strikes.

SECOND WATCHMAN
For us, never.

THE TWO OF THEM
You people above us,
your exertions are vain.
Goals evade man, they flee him
and his ever-changing aim.
He tugs and tears life's secret veil
'twixt day and night to no avail.
In vain, he seeks the sky for room;
in vain, he plumbs the deepest tomb,
and still the air retains its gloom.
Then the vault grows bright
and alternates the night
with brilliance swift in flight.
He makes his way down,
He presses ahead.
He stumbles and strays
into madness misled.

*The rear curtain opens. Decor of water and fire as in* The Magic

Flute. *Left, the fire, an elevated mound. Above, the waters, a rocky pass, but without a temple. The entire decor must be arranged in such a way that it looks as if fire and water are the only entrances to the cavern.*

### TAMINO and PAMINA

*They descend the rock with torches and sing as they climb down.*

### TAMINO

My beloved, my precious,
O how can we rescue our son;
'twixt the water and the flames,
past the monster no one tames,
rests our treasured saving grace.

*They go through the fire.*

### PAMINA

For your consort, for a mother
who is running to her youngster,
the water and the flames,
the monster no one tames,
and the guard all make a place.

*A cloud descends and floats into the center between water and fire. The cloud opens.*

### THE QUEEN OF THE NIGHT

What has happened!
Through the water, through the flame,
pressing luck in their bold mission,
up, you guards and beasts untame,
set yourselves in opposition
and protect this precious grace.

### THE WATCHMEN

*They point their spears at the casket. The lions follow them closely in attention. The arrangements on both sides should be symmetrical.*

*The Magic Flute*

We are watching, we guard the path
with spears and lion's wrath,
O Goddess, we guard your grace.

TAMINO and PAMINA (*emerging into view*)
O my husband, my beloved,
my precious, my desire,
see, the water, see, the fire
makes for mother's love a place.
You watchmen, have forbearance.

QUEEN
You watchmen, no forbearance!
Stand firmly in your place!

TAMINO and PAMINA
O woe! woe us poor parents!
Who'll save our saving grace?

QUEEN
They're storming the guarded path,
let the venging lion's wrath
devour their precious grace!

*The cloud floats away. Silence.*

THE CHILD (*in the casket*)
The voice of the father,
the mother's dear sound
is heard by the youngster
with eyes big and round.

PAMINA and TAMINO
O happiness, the first of notes.
We hear the lulling of our boy!
Don't let the magic bedazzle our joy.
You Gods! What blissfulness
blesses us both.
O let us hear once more our boy,
that sweetest note.

CHORUS (*hidden*)
Be quiet! The lad here
is no longer dozing.
The lions and spears
no longer opposing.
The cavernous snare
can't hold him inside;
he's pressing for air
with a spirited stride.

*The lid of the sarcophagus springs open. A* GENIUS *climbs out, who is completely illuminated by the lights which had made the crypt transparent. The lights must be arranged so that the upper half of the remaining figures are also luminous. The watchmen and lions suddenly enter. Tamino and Pamina withdraw.*

GENIUS
I'm here now, you loved ones!
and aren't I a joy?
Who could be saddened
to gaze at his boy?
Conceived during midnight
in the lordliest bed,
then lost to all sight
into nights filled with dread.
The pointed spears threaten,
the vengeance is seething,
the army din deafens
with dragons, fire-breathing.
Yet all of these dangers
are nothing to me.

*The instant the watchmen run at him with their spears, he flies away.*

*END OF FRAGMENT*